Re-Igniting Love and Passion

**Other Books by Guy Greenfield**

*The Wounded Parent*
*We Need Each Other*
*Self-Affirmation*
*Families Practicing God's Love*

# Re-Igniting Love and Passion

## 24 Marital Checkpoints

## Guy Greenfield

A Division of Baker Book House Co
Grand Rapids, Michigan 49516

© 1995 by Guy Greenfield

Published by Baker Books
a division of Baker Book House Company
P.O. Box 6287, Grand Rapids, MI 49516-6287

Printed in the United States of America

All rights reserved. No part of this publication may be reproduced, stored in a
retrieval system, or transmitted in any form or by any means—for example,
electronic, photocopy, recording—without the prior written permission of the
publisher. The only exception is brief quotations in printed reviews.

---

**Library of Congress Cataloging-in-Publication Data**

Greenfield, Guy
    Re-igniting love and passion : 24 marital checkpoints / Guy
Greenfield.
       p.   cm.
    ISBN 0-8010-5232-7
    1. Marriage. 2. Marriage—Religious aspects—Christianity. I. Title.
HQ734.G7395  1995
    646.7′008′655—dc20                    95-15304

---

Unless otherwise marked, Scripture is taken from the HOLY BIBLE, NEW IN-
TERNATIONAL VERSION®. NIV®. Copyright © 1973, 1978, 1984 by Interna-
tional Bible Society. Used by permission of Zondervan Publishing House. All
rights reserved.

# Contents

Preface  7

1. The Pain  11
2. The Honeymoon  17
3. The Expectations  23
4. The Needs  29
5. The Conflict  33
6. The Words  41
7. The Anger  47
8. The Fears  53
9. The Tears  59
10. The Denials  65
11. The Bedroom  71
12. The Children  77
13. The Relatives  83
14. The Job  89
15. The Finances  95
16. The Church  101
17. The Bible  107
18. The Stress  113
19. The Doctor  121
20. The Affair  127
21. The Divorce  133
22. The Reconciliation  141
23. The Counselor  147
24. The Healing  155

Questions for Discussion
in a Support Group  161
Notes  167

# Preface

When you chose to read this book, it was probably because the title spoke directly to you: The "fire" in your marriage has burned out, and you desperately wish to reignite love and passion in your relationship. Your marriage is wounded, and you feel the pain most of the time. You want help. You want healing because you are hurting.

My focus here is on healing wounded marriages. I trust that this book will also be helpful to couples, especially young married couples, in keeping their marriages healthy. It is always preferable to build strong fences at the top of a cliff than to run ambulance services at the bottom.

When considering marriages, however, I'd rather have to call for an ambulance than to call for a hearse because a marriage is dying.

What is a *wounded marriage?* I define it as an intact marriage of variable length wherein one or both partners experience a serious degree of emotional pain resulting from accumulating disappointments and discouragements in the relationship. Expectations have not been met, and it appears that they never will be if the relationship continues on its present course. Complementary needs—physical, relational, emotional, mental, and spiritual—are not being satisfactorily met.

The characteristics and symptoms of a wounded marriage include emotional pain, anger, rage, depression, infidelity, dysfunctionality, frigidity, revenge, distance, separation, confusion, rationalizations, and psychosomatic illnesses.

What is the extent of wounded marriages in American society today? My observation, study, and counseling experience suggest at least 50 percent, if not more, intact marriages are wounded to some degree. Obviously this problem contributes to the continuing high divorce rate in the United States. Also, because of continuing poor dating and courtship habits in our culture as well as the spreading of a thoroughly secular lifestyle, many more wounded marriages are on the way.

Many different things can wound a marriage. We may bring too many unrealistic and immature expectations to the marriage at the beginning. We expect too much too soon. There may also be an overemphasis on the physical, sexual, sensual, and romantic sides of marriage. Reality cannot sustain these peak experiences, so there is the inevitable letdown and disappointment.

A major contributor to a wounded marriage is poor communication. When we don't talk about our feelings and needs, misunderstandings multiply and anger and resentment may grow.

Another contributor could be a dysfunctional family of origin that poorly equipped you for a cooperative, complementary, and harmonious relationship of intimacy with your spouse. An inadequate, even dysfunctional, relationship with your parent of the opposite sex followed by a transference of those feelings from parent to spouse can damage a marriage. Expecting your marriage to meet the unmet needs and to complete the unfinished business of your childhood and looking to your spouse to solve problems that only you can solve will overload your marital circuits.

A defective moral character in one or both spouses (including a lack of honesty, truthfulness, fidelity, respect, and

# Preface

a belief in the sacredness of marriage) as well as believing that the end justifies the means could sow the seeds of marital destruction.

Other contributors to woundedness include an insensitivity to the other's feelings, a waning or cooling of the romantic dimension in the relationship with no effort at renewal, taking each other for granted, general incompatibility, a substitution of religious activity for authentic spiritual growth, and poor coping skills as the marriage undergoes stress, pressure, difficulties, and conflicts. The inability to handle stress shatters many marital dreams. This stress may be related to parenting, finances, in-laws, job situations, moving residences, overloaded schedules, or an unwillingness to talk over mutual problems.

A final, crucial contributor is a poor self-image and resultant low self-esteem that may cause you to believe, "I deserve a wounded marriage." If you really believe this, even subconsciously, you have to prove it's true by your behavior.

In this book I present a Christian perspective to this subject. I am a veteran pastor, former seminary and college professor, and marriage counselor who must be realistic about the body of believers in our society. It is my sober and unhappy judgment that there are about as many wounded marriages inside the church as there are outside.

You may think that your marriage is too far gone, even dead—it just hasn't been buried. However, a major presupposition of this author is that the God revealed in Jesus Christ is the God of resurrection. My hope is that this book may point you to the One who can both heal your wounded marriage and reignite the love and passion you once shared with your spouse.

Guy Greenfield, Ph.D.
220 Ranger Drive
Hereford, TX 79045

# 1

# The Pain

*Roberta and Steve had been married about eight years and had two children. This couple, now in their early thirties, had reached something of a stalemate in their relationship. Roberta had decided to go back to work now that the children were in school. Steve, a nuclear engineer, was desperately trying to make a favorable impression on his superiors. This involved long hours at work.*[1]

*Now that she was back at work as an interior decorator, Roberta realized that she was spending much less time with Steve. When he did come home late in the evenings and on weekends, Steve was exhausted and too tired to give Roberta or the children quality attention. Roberta said she felt like a widow with an expired yet unburied husband. Steve thought that Roberta should understand his long hours and not complain.*

*Roberta was getting more attention from male associates at work than she was from her husband at home. In time she noticed herself enjoying the flirtations of other men. The resulting guilt over such attraction and the resentment over Steve's ignoring her needs gradually became too painful to think about.*

*Jack, an attorney, was facing his fortieth birthday in a couple of months. He didn't think a lot about it, but sometimes late at night Jack was unable to sleep. He found himself staring at the ceiling and feeling that his youthfulness was slipping away from him. His wife, Donna, in her late thirties, was a good mother and homemaker; she also worked part-time for an insurance company. After eighteen years of marriage, Jack and Donna began to realize that their relationship was growing distant and stale. Their communication was minimal and shallow. Neither did anything about it, however. Under stress Jack and Donna could get into a heated argument quite easily. Their standard verbal attacks included the following:*

*Donna:*      *All you think about is sex!*
*Jack:*      *All you want from me is the money I bring home!*

*Then one day, Donna found Jack in the arms of his secretary at the office. The pain of infidelity struck deep.*

Couples in a wounded marriage know much about pain—the pain of emotional suffering rather than physical injury. Of course, hurting emotions can eventually adversely affect the body. All kinds of psychosomatic illnesses can develop among those who have a wounded marriage. Mind and emotions *(psycho)* can have considerable power over the body *(somatic),* either for good or for ill, depending on the nature of the thoughts and feelings. Authors Norman Cousins, Bernie Siegel, and Blair Justice have thoroughly documented and explained this close interworking of mind and body.[2] However, I wish to focus here on the nonphysical type of pain—those feelings of anguish that medicine does not so easily eliminate.

This is the pain you feel when you begin to perceive your marriage as a serious disappointment; when you notice that you are regretting having ever married your spouse; when

# The Pain

your earliest feelings of joy, thrill, pleasure, and happiness are no longer or rarely ever felt.

This is the pain you experience when special days are no longer remembered by your spouse. Your wedding anniversary passes by without comment. Your birthday was just another date on the calendar this past year. If you have small children, your spouse did not take the initiative to assist them to surprise you with something special on Mother's Day or Father's Day.

You may be hanging in there, hoping that the relationship will improve, that significant changes will take place, and that the pain will gradually go away. But so far none of this has happened. Possibly the pain seems to get worse by the week. However, you really don't want a divorce; you want to make this marriage work someway, somehow.

I think it helps to identify the nature of the pain felt in a wounded marriage. We have a reservoir of words in the English language that describe pain and related feelings:

| | | |
|---|---|---|
| suffering | anguish | ache |
| distress | disturbed | cramp |
| grief | tormented | tortured |
| soreness | sorrow | woe |
| misery | pang | troubled |
| worried | angry | embarrassed |
| contentious | repressed | anxious |
| repulsive | touchy | melancholy |
| rageful | panicky | horrified |
| nauseated | irritated | stretched |
| stressful | fearful | belligerent |
| disgusted | alarmed | depressed |
| paralyzed | uptight | locked up |
| trapped | tense | scared |
| terrified | powerless | defiant |
| low | lonely | threatened |
| sweaty | tired | beaten |

| | | |
|---|---|---|
| burdened | weepy | bushed |
| taut | heavy | jealous |
| sad | helpless | impotent |
| impatient | played out | bored |
| down | end of your rope | frustrated |
| cold | hot | hurt |
| rejected | resentful | confused |
| unwanted | unneeded | unloved |
| disappointed | discouraged | despondent |

Now take a pencil and circle the words that come closest to describing how you feel about your marriage at this time. These terms could aid you in recognizing the symptoms of a wounded marriage. This list is not intended to cause you additional pain but rather to enable you to get a handle on your feelings so you can take charge of them. Scattered throughout this book are suggestions regarding how to do this.

In discussing the pain of a wounded marriage, I am in no way overlooking the fact that not *all* aspects of such a marriage are painful. There have in all likelihood been many good times and enjoyable experiences in the years you have been together as husband and wife. It is important to affirm to yourself that it hasn't all been bad. Very likely the good times actually outweigh the bad. If that were not so, you probably would have divorced by now.

The fact that you are still living together suggests that you still want this marriage to work, to recapture those good feelings and happy times you had in the marriage's earlier days, and to find constructive ways to deal with the many negatives that tend to spoil the relationship. In case you are not living together at this time, you may want to find a way to get back together again.

It is very important to remember that not all pain is bad or undesirable. Some physical pain serves as a warning that something in your body is wrong and in need of treatment. The same can be true in a relationship that is hurting. The

# The Pain

pain of a wounded marriage can point us to areas in the relationship that need to be changed, repaired, strengthened, or enriched. The wounds can also point to aspects of your personality that may need to be altered in some way.

A heavy dose of disappointment in your marriage may call for some revision in unrealistic expectations. If you are experiencing a lot of anger toward your spouse, you may need to learn new skills for controlling your emotional responses.

*Joanne had been an only child who had received considerable attention and recognition from her parents and grandparents. As a married adult she expected to receive the same level of attention and recognition to which she had been accustomed as a child, but her husband, Ben, did not satisfy her high expectations because he was so busy developing his profession. Her response was the pain of disappointment.*

*Susan had learned early in life that she could control people around her with anger. Now as a married adult, she tried to control her husband, Joel, with anger when he balked at going to church on Sunday. A steady dose of anger resulted in the pain of an angry disposition and the loss of tenderness and intimacy.*

What can you do about pain in a wounded marriage? The best response is to make it a learning experience. Then you set about making the necessary changes. This does not mean you try to change your spouse—a very unproductive strategy. You can only change yourself! You can change your perception, your evaluation, and your responses. But a change within yourself will invariably have an effect on the situation.

Only masochists enjoy pain. Realists consider pain as a symptom of something gone wrong. They see it as a warning regarding a problem that needs immediate attention. Pain is not only a sign of needed change, but it is also an invitation to growth. This book is written for the wounded marriage of the couple who desires to grow beyond the pain.

# 2

# The Honeymoon

Wounded marriages are prone to live in the pain of the present. Any thoughts about previous times in the relationship tend to dwell on the conflict and unhappy experiences; the good times are so easily overlooked or forgotten. Every couple in a wounded marriage needs to reflect back on their honeymoon in an effort to recapture, at least mentally, something of the ecstasy of those first days of harmony and joy that followed their wedding.

Have you ever tried to describe to an intimate friend what happened on your honeymoon? I say *intimate* since not all of your friends would necessarily want to hear about it, and you would want to share the details of those days only with one of your closest confidants. But it would be a good exercise for someone in a wounded marriage to talk about those first days of marriage. Sharing an event may help you to recover something of the original feelings.

I suppose every honeymoon is unique and special. Also, I imagine that every honeymoon has both its positives and its negatives—no honeymoon is idyllic. Many couples have

18 Re-Igniting Love and Passion

no idea what to expect. Expectations may even be too high, which could ruin or diminish the joy of even a normal honeymoon (whatever that is).

*When Carole and I married, we were fairly young and "green as grass." I turned twenty-one three days into our honeymoon, while she was barely nineteen. We had no idea what to expect. We married on August 14 in hot, pre-air-conditioning, southwestern Oklahoma. We immediately headed for the cool mountains of Colorado—Denver to be exact. In those days before freeways, that amounted to a long drive over hot terrain. If I had had any sense, we would have planned a shorter trip. Most of our time was spent in the car going somewhere.*

*Denver was nice, although it was not as cool as we had expected. We arrived there on a Saturday afternoon and attended church the next morning. The atmosphere in that particular church was cooler than the weather. The sermon was dull; no one spoke to us. That afternoon we enjoyed walking through Denver's beautiful city park near downtown. We visited some museums, the state capitol building, and other historic places. But we spent a lot of time in our motel room getting acquainted sexually—both of us scared, excited, and clumsy. Frankly, we overdid it, but we were too stupid and naive to know what to do. We were kids trying to be instant adults. But that's all right. You have to start somewhere, and we had a lot of fun.*

*However, on our way back to Oklahoma, driving between Raton and Clayton, New Mexico, we got into our first big argument. I really don't remember how it started. I do recall it had something to do with finances. We were in college and had a long road of schooling ahead of us. Carole was raised to spend whatever money you had, while I was reared to save as much as possible. I just knew she was going to spend us into financial obliteration, and she thought I was turning into a tightwad. Our inexperience and insecurities almost ruined the trip before we got back to our apartment at college.*

*Those first months were not as pleasant as we had thought they would be. We had no training, education, or experience regarding married life. But then who does? We miraculously stumbled through*

# The Honeymoon

*those early days of "wedded bliss." After forty-three years, we both look back and wonder how we made it. We didn't know it then, but we were so different. We came out of considerably different family backgrounds. Our personalities had major differences that could easily set us up for conflict on a moment's notice. What was worse, we honestly didn't know why. We didn't understand the dynamics at work in our conflicts.*

*I find it a good experience to go back from time to time and look through our wedding album of pictures and stir up the good memories of those first days of our marriage. One of the most precious photographs we have is one of the two of us standing beside our 1948 Plymouth soon after returning from our honeymoon. We look like two skinny teenagers hooked on puppy love. We both have changed so much physically since then that no one would recognize us. Looking at those pictures taken in 1952, I am reminded that what brought us together has somehow kept us together through these many years. I would describe that as a covenant love commitment that was rooted in a common faith relationship with Jesus Christ as Lord of our lives and our marriage.*

What about couples whose honeymoon and early marriage memories are more unpleasant than pleasant? I have had some couples tell me that their honeymoon was either a nightmare or at least a major disappointment. The relationship suffered what was perceived to be a major setback early on. Some never seemed to get over it.

One young woman told me that she realized on their first wedding night that she had made a mistake in her choice of a husband. Men can have the same experience. One college graduate student told me, "On our wedding night I discovered that I had married a frigid woman." A schoolteacher shared with me that during their engagement her fiancé had been nothing but a gentleman, but on their wedding night his approach to sex was crude, rude, and vulgar. She could not understand how getting married could change a man into a seemingly different person.

Not many couples who have such early disappointing experiences survive their first year. Research shows that the first year of marriage is truly a crucial time for any couple.[3] If you fit the category of the survivor of early disappointments in marriage, what do you do now? Well, you have probably made considerable adjustments or you wouldn't still be married. Yet a major problem in your current situation may be the lingering unpleasant memories of the past. There is only one solution: a combination of understanding and forgiveness of what happened.

The unhappiness of your honeymoon and early months of marriage may still be eating at your insides. You may be holding a grudge and expressing deep resentment over your disappointment in marrying this particular person. Such persistent anger accomplishes nothing and only makes life miserable for both of you. This is a situation where a trained counselor can assist you to bring these long-standing resentments out into the open in a search for understanding exactly what happened and possibly why. (See chapter 23 for further discussion of the benefits of marriage counseling at the hands of a competent and skilled therapist.)

Only when the anger and disappointment are openly dealt with can forgiveness be mustered, expressed, and accepted. You surely love each other to some degree or you wouldn't still be married. One of the most significant and practical expressions of love is forgiveness, and there is something to forgive in every marriage relationship. Sometimes that something needing forgiveness goes way back to the first days of your marriage. There is such a thing as a *toxic marriage*. What makes it toxic is a persisting attitude of an unforgiving spirit.

Your disappointment may not be over anything major like infidelity. It may instead focus on a number of annoying and irritating personal habits:

# The Honeymoon

- leaving the lid off the toothpaste tube
- leaving clothes strewn around the bedroom
- snoring
- ignoring dirty dishes on the table
- never offering to help with basic chores around the house or apartment
- lack of tenderness or sensitivity to your feelings
- making a lot of noise early in the morning while the other is trying to sleep
- consistently failing to record checks in the checkbook
- making fun of your failures
- using vulgar language
- thoughtlessly smoking around nonsmokers
- drinking too much
- regularly complaining about other people's actions
- always expressing a negative view
- bad table manners

Everyone can make their own list of irritants. These must be dealt with at the right time and in the right place, possibly with the help of a skillful counselor, so that minor irritants do not become a major threat to your marriage.

The honeymoon is over, the early days of marriage are past, and you cannot go back and relive them with new resolve to make things different. You have to start where you are. If those first days of marriage were wonderful, marvelous, exciting, and joyful but things have gone downhill since then (or at least in recent months), go back in your memories and try to recapture the mood and remember why you got married in the first place. If those first days were a major disappointment, do some reevaluation of what happened and attempt to understand the possible causes while administering a heavy dose of forgiveness.

For some of you the past may need to be recovered; for others it may need to be resolved. Recover the strength of its joys; deal constructively with the weaknesses of its mistakes. If used properly, the past can offer hope for a better future in your marriage. Wounded marriages can be healed!

# 3

# The Expectations

Most marriages begin with hopeful expectations. Yet those expectations are not always clear in our minds; some are even subconscious. We expect our marriage to bring fulfillment to all our hopes and dreams for a meaningful relationship. More specifically, in Harville Hendrix's words, marriage is "getting the love you want."[4]

Dr. Hendrix, a Dallas and New York based psychotherapist, proposes an interesting and practical theory: Couples marry in a subconscious attempt to resolve the conflicts of their childhood, to complete the "unfinished business"[5] of their past. Each of us subconsciously believes that his or her spouse will bring all the answers to the unsolved problems of the early years of life. This attempt to resolve your past is called by Hendrix "the unconscious marriage." The problem with this is that many try to make a marriage work without changing the approaches and behavior patterns learned in the past. But if we haven't resolved our past by our wedding day, it isn't likely we will do so after marrying if we continue using the old approaches and behavior patterns.

Hendrix recommends a radically different type of marriage—"the conscious marriage," a relationship that helps you to satisfy your unmet childhood needs in positive ways that primarily emphasize cooperation rather than conflict, mutual growth and support rather than confrontation and criticism.[6]

When the expectations you brought with you into your marriage are not fulfilled, you are likely to respond with disappointment, discouragement, and pain. A wounded marriage results. Of course, the primary mistake here is that you are looking to someone else to complete the unfinished business of your childhood, to resolve your early childhood conflicts, and to make you happy.

*Several years ago Carl and Sue attended a marriage enrichment leadership training workshop. One of the exercises they were asked to do involved taking a crayon and writing on a large sheet of paper the words they had never heard but always wanted to hear from their parent of the opposite sex. They were also asked to write with their left hand if they were right-handed or use their right hand if they were left-handed. This was to simulate the writing of a child since they were recalling unheard but longed-for words of their childhood.*

*Both Carl and Sue found the exercise extremely difficult and painful. It took Carl a long time to pull up the words he had always wanted to hear from his mother. She had been a basically good mother, a devout Christian, a hardworking person, and a faithful church worker. She had died several years before, and now Carl tended to idealize her. It was an inner struggle to call up anything that could be interpreted as a criticism of her.*

*Eventually the words came: "That was a very good job, son; I'm very proud of you." Carl had wanted to hear her unconditional affirmation of him. She tended to say something like, "I enjoyed what you said, but . . ." Then she would add some conditional criticism. Even when Carl became an adult, and a pastor at that (something she had always hoped for from at least one of her sons),*

# The Expectations

*Carl never quite preached to suit her expectations. For example, he "never preached enough on love." He "didn't pray enough." (Carl always wondered how she knew how much he prayed.) He "didn't visit the sick enough." His mother was full of advice. Carl knew she was well-intentioned, but it came across as telling him that he didn't quite measure up to her expectations. There wasn't much supportive affirmation.*

*So Carl came into his marriage with Sue expecting her to make up for his mother's shortcomings. He looked to his wife to give him the affirmation his mother never quite gave him. Of course, Sue didn't know this, and when she didn't affirm Carl to the degree that he expected, he felt deeply disappointed.*

*Since Sue is not naturally an affirming person, this revelation was difficult for her. She had grown up with a critical, somewhat perfectionistic mind-set herself. Affirmation was not a usual part of her response to others. Oh, she could give compliments, but they had to be well earned in an unusually special event or performance.*

*When Sue tried to recall words she most wanted to hear from her father, it was a difficult experience for her as well. Sue's father had always been a steady, faithful husband and father in their family. Although he had his faults like everyone else, he was a down-to-earth, good man. However, at home he was the quiet type and not the big decision maker when it came to the children. Mother was the one in charge there. She was what Hugh Missildine calls an "over coercive" parent.[7] Although a good woman in so many ways, she could be very heavy-handed with control. Sue felt that she never had much freedom of choice or independence of thinking.*

*Consequently, Sue had always wanted to hear from her father the words: "I take Sue's side in this matter. I think she is right in wanting to do this. I think she should have that freedom." Rather, Dad would say, "Ask your mother. You have to do whatever she says." Sue felt that her father was not the advocate, supporter, and defender he could have been on her behalf.*

*Consequently, when Sue married Carl, she naturally looked to her husband to make up for what her father had not been to her. She looked to Carl to be supportive, defending, and protective of her.*

*She expected him to give her the freedom she seldom had at home with her parents. Both Carl and Sue expected the other to finish their unfinished business from childhood. When this did not happen, both experienced uncomfortableness, discontent, and sometimes even pain. A wounded marriage gradually developed.*

My wife and I have administered this exercise to numerous couples in marriage enrichment retreats we have led over the past several years. We never fail to be amazed how many couples discover something similar to what Carl and Sue learned about themselves. A wounded marriage is so often the result of shattered expectations.

What expectations did you bring into your marriage? Take a pen and paper and write down some of them. As you see them in a list, you will be able to look at them more objectively. Next, take each expectation individually and ask yourself how realistic and fair it is. Perhaps you have been transferring unfulfilled expectations of your childhood to your spouse, looking to him or her to make up for what your parents didn't or couldn't provide.

Ask yourself if it is fair to expect your spouse to do for you what your parents didn't do. You are now a grown, married adult with full responsibility for yourself. Could it be that it is now time for you to meet some of these expectations for yourself?

For example, let's say that your parents didn't recognize or affirm you enough when you were a child. Now you are looking to your spouse to supply the affirmation and recognition you feel you need. Instead of putting all that heavy load on him or her, why not give yourself some self-recognition or self-affirmation? Aren't you by now a pretty good judge of your abilities, accomplishments, and character traits? Then learn to stroke yourself. Oh, it would be nice for your spouse or some significant other to give you strokes, but you don't really need it from them. Learn to affirm yourself. If you are constantly looking to someone else to give

# The Expectations

you a sense of worth or importance, you could be setting yourself up for a lot of unnecessary disappointment.

If you have a wounded marriage along these lines, you may be overloading your marital circuits by too many unrealistic and even unfair expectations. It doesn't hurt to share your expectations with your spouse if it can be mutual. Then work to provide a measure of what your spouse expects of you. But don't expect someone else to do for you what you can do for yourself. The process of maturity involves the maturation of your expectations as well. To paraphrase the apostle Paul, "When I became an adult, I put away childish expectations" (see 1 Cor. 13:11).

Wounded marriages are often the result of disappointment over unfulfilled expectations. Therefore, such expectations need to be reevaluated and reprioritized. This marital hidden agenda may need to be brought out into the open, examined, and revised. Moreover, it will help a great deal to move your concentration of concern off yourself and focus more on your spouse. He or she may be seriously disappointed also. Being lovingly and caringly sensitive to the feelings of your spouse is the first step to healing a wounded marriage. Licking your own wounds and feeling sorry for yourself is not productive in healing a relationship.

# 4

## The Needs

Everyone has needs. Physically, each of us needs food, rest, exercise, and the other normal functioning of our bodily processes. Mentally, we need to think, understand, and reason, and our minds need to exercise some meaningful language and communication in the context of our culture. Emotionally, we need the freedom to express our feelings in a healthy and balanced manner. Spiritually, we need some kind of purpose and direction for life that goes beyond simply the here and now. Relationally, we need other persons in wholesome, interpersonal relationships.

Sometimes we get *needs* and *wants* mixed up. What we want, we may not really need. A new car, a new house, more clothes, a better job, or more money may be desirable and even enjoyable, but they may not necessarily be needed at this time. Needs have to do with keeping us whole, balanced, and satisfied to an acceptable degree. Obviously I am not referring to what might be called bare survival needs. If you were shipwrecked on a South Seas island all alone, you might be able to survive on a lot less than you would be willing to settle for back in civilization. Rather, I am referring to normal, everyday functioning needs in the context of your present situation.

When you got married, you had certain needs that you hoped would be met in your marriage. As suggested in the previous chapter, the expectations you bring to your marriage, whether conscious or not, involve certain basic needs that you anticipate will be met by your spouse.

The wounded marriage usually is one in which the perceived needs of one or both of the partners are not being met to an acceptable degree. As I think back over the hundreds of couples I have counseled over the past several years, I must conclude that they initially came to me for counseling because some of their primary needs were not being adequately met in their marriage. Their pain was the pain of emotional and relational deprivation in the relationship.

Dr. Willard F. Harley Jr., a clinical psychologist in Minnesota, has written a fascinating yet practical book regarding need-meeting in marriage.[8] His research and conclusions confirm my own observations. From years of experience with numerous couples, Dr. Harley has identified ten basic human needs within the marriage relationship. When he asked men and women to prioritize their needs, he discovered that the top five needs of men and the top five needs of women were totally different. Of course, individuals perceive their needs differently, but overall, the statistical ranking by hundreds of persons answering Harley's questionnaire revealed the following results:

A husband's five most basic needs in marriage were

1. sexual fulfillment
2. recreational companionship
3. an attractive spouse
4. domestic support
5. admiration

# The Needs 31

A wife's five most basic needs in marriage were

1. affection
2. conversation
3. honesty and openness
4. financial support
5. family commitment

Keep in mind that both men and women have all ten of these needs. Yet what the husbands considered their most important needs tended to be what the wives ranked as least important, and vice versa. Since husbands and wives typically have different needs, it is necessary for both men and women to make serious attempts to work at making relational adjustments in their marriage.

When a wife works to provide her husband sexual fulfillment on a regular and consistent basis; recreational companionship—sharing with him in whatever he does for fun and relaxation; an attractive spouse in looks and behavior; domestic support—taking adequate care of home and children; and admiration—encouragement, support, and affirmation; she will find a much more contented husband who will be sufficiently, even enthusiastically, satisfied with his marriage. Such contentment and satisfaction will provide a shield from any serious consideration of ever desiring another woman.

Likewise, when a husband concentrates on providing his wife with affection—generally nonsexual forms involving words, attitude, deeds, even little considerations such as tenderness and thoughtfulness; conversation—with emphasis on attentive listening more than verbal comments; honesty and openness—a woman cannot tolerate a dishonest and secretive man; financial support—even though she may choose to work, a wife needs to know that if necessary her husband can be the primary provider regardless of what she does about her time outside the home; and family commitment—she needs to know that her husband's sole commitment is to their family and to no one or nothing else; then he will observe a much more contented wife who will in all likelihood be very satisfied with her marriage. This degree of contentment and satisfaction will provide such a husband with a guarantee that his wife will have no interest in any other man.

Wounded marriages tend to be those that do not work to meet these basic needs. They are need-hungry—starving for what the marriage does not provide. Similar to nutritional deficiency, such marriages suffer from need-provision deficiency. The sad thing about this is that most of these wounded spouses are ignorant of what is wrong with the marriage.

If your relationship with your spouse has some of the characteristics of a wounded marriage, you should take a mental survey of your needs—both yours and those of your spouse. Look over Harley's needs list again. How would you prioritize your list?

Invite your spouse to participate in an exercise with you. Begin by listing what you each perceive to be your spouse's primary needs. Then exchange lists for the purpose of re-ordering the priorities and adding needs that were left off. Then exchange lists again and discuss the discrepancies. Be open and honest in explaining each need listed, being as specific and concrete as possible. Give examples of each need to illustrate exactly what you mean.

For the next several days, make every effort to meet these needs that have now been brought to your attention. If both of you will cooperate and work hard, I can guarantee you that you will see an immediate improvement in your relationship. When each is committed to meeting the needs of the other, a rewarding, harmonious enthusiasm will permeate the relationship. Don't worry about getting your own needs met—the selfish focus doesn't work. Concentrate on meeting your spouse's needs. If both of you do this, each will experience the other's love in an extremely practical way. And that kind of love will grow!

# 5

# The Conflict

A wounded marriage is usually a conflicted marriage. Some marriages have even been identified as "conflict habituated" by family sociologists. These marriages seem to thrive on conflict. They consider conflict to be the normal atmosphere for day-to-day "marital breathing." If there were no conflict in their marriage, these couples would think that something was wrong, that one or the other was sick, or that their spouse didn't care about or love them anymore.

Studies show that conflict habituated marriages tend to be a union of persons who grew up in a family atmosphere of both conflict and strong commitment. Conflict was a part of their normal cultural behavior pattern. It was subconsciously considered a technique for survival, yet they would seldom consider separation or divorce. Such persons are considered naturally choleric, irascible, and hot-tempered. They do not regard their behavior as abnormal or dangerous to their relationship, especially if both of the couple are of such temperament. They would rather "fight than switch."

However, most of us are not choleric. We find conflict neither pleasant nor acceptable. We would rather switch than fight; at least we would rather retreat than fight. We usually choose to avoid conflict if at all possible. Conflict is generally perceived as having a negative impact and a destructive effect. Most couples have experienced their share of arguments, but a wounded marriage is one that has known an undue amount of verbal fighting.

*Jeff and Melissa started their marriage like any pair of young lovebirds. They were attracted to each other for several reasons and felt truly in love with each other. There was the obvious physical attraction, but Melissa and Jeff had other commonalities, mostly in the realm of religion: same church, same beliefs, same moral values. "Two good Baptist kids ought to make a good marriage," their pastor told them.*

*Yet Jeff and Melissa fought almost from the beginning. Their arguments, it seemed to them, were often over the most trivial matters. Money was at the heart of many of their disagreements. Jeff had been raised in a financially conservative home and taught that money was to be saved. Melissa was raised in a financially poor family and was taught that what little money you had ought to be spent before it got away from you. In one sense, Melissa's family believed that spending money was one way to gain a sense of security, because they believed that surrounding yourself with food, furniture, clothes (especially clothes), and anything others could see, proved that "you had it." Material possessions convey security; having nothing means insecurity.*

*Jeff's family struggled with a business during the harsh 1930s depression. Money in the bank was the best way to stave off the bill collectors and to protect yourself from the dangers of poverty, which were always just around the corner. The way to accumulate money (and thus security) was to save it, not spend it.*

*So when Melissa sought to spend Jeff's hard-earned and meticulously saved money, a verbal battle ensued. Jeff felt threatened that Melissa would spend him into poverty. Melissa felt that Jeff was*

# The Conflict                                    35

*a tightwad who loved money more than he loved her. The conflict was one of different values and emotions that surprisingly did not emerge during their dating and engagement.*

*Sex was another battle arena for this couple. For Jeff sex was a primary way to give and receive love in marriage. Having been deprived of much demonstrative love as a child, he discovered after marriage that sex was one way to feel that he was truly loved. However, Melissa viewed sex as a moral black hole. Her mother had implicitly taught her to fear sex. For a single girl it was one sure way to "get into trouble"—mostly with mother, of course. To get pregnant as a single teenager was an unpardonable sin. Indirectly, her mother had conveyed that sex was basically dirty, dangerous, and disgusting. These inhibitions her mother had programmed into Melissa were not easily thrown off with a wedding ring.*

*However, the problem for Melissa was bigger than sex. She had been so smothered with affection by her mother and other relatives as a child that demonstrations of affection (kissing and hugging) tended to mean one thing: control. Moreover, Melissa's father was never demonstrative in his love for her. His aloofness communicated one thing to his daughter: indifference. He felt he showed love by bringing home a paycheck each week, coming home at 5:00 P.M. each day, and fixing things around the house. Since mother was in charge of the children, father kept his distance from them so far as demonstrative affection. That was mother's job.*

*So when Jeff and Melissa married, Melissa was not very affectionate, and she felt sex should be mostly for having children. Jeff was expecting physical demonstrations of love, and if he seemed demanding about sex, Melissa balked, and conflict was under way. It did not take long for theirs to become a wounded marriage.*

A marriage is a lot like the human heart. It needs sufficient oxygen to function properly. When the marriage's arteries become clogged emotionally and psychologically, the heart of the marriage will soon be in serious trouble. When the personal needs of a couple are not being met in the relationship, a marital heart attack is a strong possibility. Just as it takes time for arteries to clog, so it takes time for a marriage to deteriorate. When the interpersonal needs of a couple are not met over a period of years, marital heart damage is inevitable.

Conflict in a marriage is one clear sign that some of the basic needs of the couple are not being met. These primary needs were elaborated upon in the previous chapter. Go back and reread what Dr. Harley found regarding those needs and ask yourself what need deprivation in your marriage might be contributing to conflict in your relationship. What needs of your spouse are you not meeting? If you're drawing a blank on this, ask your spouse to help you. Completing the sentence: "At this time in our marriage, I need _____" could help prime the pump for meaningful discussion.

However, keep in mind that no marriage is always conflict free. Conflict is normal. Conflict is inevitable. Conflict is human. But conflict is resolvable. There are a lot of areas for conflict in a marriage. In addition to money and sex, there are differences over parenting techniques, religious views and church attendance, political ideology, job changes, residential location, vacation plans, in-law relations, choice of friends, as well as basic misunderstanding about something that was said. But there are usually emotional roots beneath the conflict regardless of what the conflict is about. These roots can sometimes be found when a couple is willing to work through the stages of conflict resolution. Commitment to resolve the conflict is an absolute essential here.

The following steps can help:[9]

1. *Try to discover the nature of the problem.* Calm down, back off from a conflict stance, stop making threats, and use your common sense to assess the reasons for the conflict. Being calm in your conversation here can help immensely,

# The Conflict

especially if you will learn to use *I* messages instead of *you* messages.[10]

For example, you might use *I* messages and say:

> "I really think I need some time to calm down and think about what is going on here. I really do love you, but I don't understand what's going on between us right now. I'm really upset by our fighting over this, and when I get my anger under control, I believe I can be more reasonable."

rather than *you* messages:

> "You stupid idiot, don't you know that if you had even the brain of a flea you could see that I'm right after all? You're the cause of the trouble here because you are so selfish and egotistical. This entire fight is your fault. Now you listen to me. . . ."

In addition, if you'll give one another a chance, you might discover that one of you has a physical/medical problem (normal complications with a woman's menstrual cycle can sometimes be the irritant behind a marital conflict) or an emotional problem (grief over the loss of a parent, a child, or a job). One of you may be struggling with a big financial problem (not enough money to pay all the bills), while the other may have recently lost face in a social situation (bypassed for a promotion or didn't get elected president of a club or chairman of the church board). In other words, the immediate conflict is sometimes the symptom of a deeper disturbance that is not always obvious.

2. *Utilize open lines of communication.* There is no simple way to do this. Thomas Gordon's suggestions for *active listening* can be a productive approach to learn.[11] Stop trying to make your point so you can win the argument and start listening to the views and feelings of your spouse. You can open lines of communication by backing away from an aggressive, judgmental, or argumentative stance, kindly ex-

pressing your feelings while inviting the other to do likewise, reflecting what you're hearing in friendly and fresh language to see if you really understand, and even using the loving touch (holding a hand, a hug, a hand on the shoulder, an arm around the other) to communicate your concern for your spouse.

3. *Commit yourself to work through the eight stages of conflict resolution:*

1. Contention—something produces strife.
2. Condemnation—accusations are made.
3. Confusion—participants are at a loss to know what to do. (Note: You are probably at this stage when you recognize the need for conflict resolution.)
4. Confrontation—one of you recommends that the two of you sit down and look things over, possibly with a third party.
5. Consideration—each seriously considers the other's views.
6. Communication—feelings, viewpoints, and goals are freely shared with *I* messages.
7. Conciliation—mutual concessions and compromises are made.
8. Cooperation—agreement to work together in spite of differences and the past.

4. *Go for help if the situation appears to be beyond your ability to cope.* A competent, well-trained, Christian professional counselor may be able to bring clarity and sanity to your situation.

Persistent, ongoing, unresolved conflict can wound any marriage. You probably do not understand why the conflict continues, nor do you know what to do about it. But remember, a marriage in conflict does not need to be destroyed; it needs to be healed. One of the basic steps in heal-

# The Conflict

39

ing a wounded marriage is to learn how to resolve conflict whenever it arises. To this point in your life, you probably did not learn many constructive conflict-resolution skills. That is what this book is partially about. You will see this as we move through the remainder of the chapters.

# 6

# The Words

Many of the wounds found in a wounded marriage are inflicted by harsh and spiteful words. The old adage, "Sticks and stones may break my bones, but words will never harm me," is simply not true.

Words are powerful. They express ideas, beliefs, values, feelings, tastes, hopes and dreams, and decisions. People in wounded marriages tend to remember a lot of words—some spoken hastily, others thoughtlessly, and still others in anger, grief, or pain.

*Marsha and Lynn came for counseling after they finally grew weary of all the arguing. Their marriage was characterized by argumentative words—a seemingly constant barrage of attempts to prove that one was right and the other was wrong. Both could not be right all of the time, and both could not be wrong all of the time, but each insisted that his or her own viewpoint was the only correct one, never seeking to understand the other's views or wishes.*

*This couple had been married for six years, and Marsha believed it was time to start a family. Even though both had by now finished college, Lynn still felt that they needed to save more money before having their first baby. Besides, having a baby would mean Marsha would have to stop work for a time, and that would mean less income. When Marsha said "baby," Lynn would respond "not yet."*

*After a year of putting her off, Lynn became irritated whenever Marsha would raise the issue. The arguments began. The words flowed—accusations, charges and countercharges, threats, intimidations, anger, and resentment. A recent conversation:*

| | |
|---|---|
| *Marsha:* | *Lynn, you told me when we married that you wanted a family.* |
| *Lynn:* | *Yes, but we're not ready yet.* |
| *Marsha:* | *After six years! I'm out of school and have earned a good income these past two years, much of which we have saved.* |
| *Lynn:* | *But that's not enough. Don't you know how expensive it is to have a baby?* |
| *Marsha:* | *But it's not going to get any less expensive the longer we wait. Besides, our medical insurance will cover most of the hospital and doctors' bills.* |
| *Lynn:* | *Yes, but that's only a small part of paying for a family.* |
| *Marsha:* | *So when will we ever know we're ready and can afford it? Just how much money will we need to have saved before we can start?* |
| *Lynn:* | *I don't know exactly how much. Don't pin me down to details like that. I'll let you know when we're ready. Don't bother me about this any more.* |
| *Marsha:* | *(crying) I feel like you're never going to be ready. If you really loved me, you'd do what I want about this.* |
| *Lynn:* | *Are you saying that I don't love you?* |
| *Marsha:* | *Yes, I don't think you truly love me!* |

# The Words    43

| | |
|---|---|
| *Lynn:* | *Well, thanks a lot! Maybe you don't love me either since you want to push us into debt with a bunch of snotty-nosed kids!* |
| *Marsha:* | *(crying and shouting) So that's how you really feel about children! I suspected as much. Now the ugly truth is out. You lied to me about wanting children!* |

*So the battle of words went on and on and on. Many of the words in Marsha and Lynn's dialogue were like spears, piercing the soul of their relationship. Words like these spoken in frustration, anger, fear, disappointment, or intimidation are wounding words, often leaving deep emotional scars. Some of the wounds never really heal but continue to bleed and ooze with continuing resentment.*

*Until Marsha and Lynn came for counseling, they never seemed to understand the reasoning (or lack of it) behind their verbal battles. They did not perceive the emotional dynamics underlying their thoughts and speech. Their conversations about their family's future lacked insight and never reached any agreement.*

*In this case, Marsha's desire to start their family certainly seemed normal and expected. However, Lynn's fears and insecurity seemed abnormal and unwarranted, given the facts. Although his fears and insecurity had probably been there all along, deeply rooted in his psyche by certain early childhood experiences, Lynn did not know why he felt the way he did. He sought to defend himself with words that were sharp and cruel overreactions to a perceived economic threat, and those words wounded the marriage at a critical point in the relationship.*

*It took Marsha a long time to get over these verbal injuries. It was only as this couple learned in counseling how to work through their feelings, control their choice of words, and direct their conversations toward mutual understanding in reaching common goals that the healing of past wounds took place.*

*Words can never harm me?* Experience for most of us proves otherwise. Words can be very damaging because they can symbolize conflict, attack, resentment, rejection, and threat. If words are not meant to harm, they can nevertheless be taken or perceived to be harmful when spoken carelessly and harshly.

Sometimes we do not really mean what we say. We speak in frustration and anger before we think. But such words when taken at face value, combined with a certain tone of voice, facial expression, and body language, can carry a strong message that was not intended.

There are times when our words are misunderstood. They are confused, vague, or poorly chosen. The words are spoken when we are physically tired and exhausted or when we are ill and worn out. We may be trying to say, "I don't feel good," or, "I'm not sure what is going on here," or, "I need time to think this over," but our words don't come out exactly that way. They are taken with a different meaning than intended. Such miscommunication can result in verbal wounds.

Have you ever found yourself shouting at your spouse, "Leave me alone!" or "I hate you!" or something worse, when in reality you were tired and worn out from extra long and tedious hours at work? Or you may have been angry at your boss or a colleague at work, and you came home and dumped your anger on the one you love. Yet the damage was done. The words, although misdirected, still wounded your spouse, who did not understand or who may have retaliated with equally wounding words.

Many couples need a year in "marital language school" much like missionaries who are appointed to serve overseas need a year of special language training. Healthy marriages are largely based on knowing the language of marital relationships. This language is different from the language of commerce, school, church, or politics.

Healthy marital language is one of consideration, mutual respect, clarity, consistency, love, fun, honesty, thoughtfulness, kindness, and truthfulness. It is always preceded by at-

# The Words

tentive listening and understanding of each other's emotions and current experiences. For those of us who didn't learn this in our family of origin, hard work and serious commitment to learning good communication skills are required. All married couples could benefit from reading Thomas Gordon's discussion of the difference between *you* messages and *I* messages in his book *Parent Effectiveness Training*.[12] Although the subject of the book is parenting, the communication principles apply equally to marriage.

Damage control for wounding words may call for professional counseling to work through the pain and achieve healing and renewal. Such counseling will help a couple to gain insight into why there is an inclination to lash out at the one you married whenever pressure and stress are experienced. Retraining in conversation may be needed in addition to understanding and controlling the emotions behind your words.

Healing for wounded marriages may begin with learning the art of speaking healing words:

- questions that seek honest understanding
- statements of encouragement
- comments of affirmation
- remarks of affection
- requests for clarification
- reassurances of love and appreciation
- willingness to achieve consensus through compromises and adjustments
- reflections of hope
- confessions of wrong spirit or actions
- requests for and/or granting of forgiveness
- professions of recommitment and solidarity in the relationship

- expressions of healthy humor (at your own expense) when you can honestly laugh at yourself
- the use of honest *I* messages rather than judgmental *you* messages

Words in themselves are neutral. It is how they are used that matters. Wounded marriages are often wounded by ill-chosen and ill-timed words. But wounded marriages can be healed by the use of healing words that flow from a healthy heart.

The sage declared, "Above all else, guard your heart, for it is the wellspring of life" (Prov. 4:23). Jesus taught that what corrupts a person comes from within, not from without (see Mark 7:20–23), and this could apply to a marriage as well. He also taught that

> out of the overflow of the heart the mouth speaks. . . . But I tell you that men will have to give account on the day of judgment for every careless word they have spoken. For by your words you will be acquitted, and by your words you will be condemned.
>
> Matthew 12:34, 36–37

And who can forget James's teaching about the potential for good or evil in the words we speak (see James 3:1–12). Therefore, the healing of a wounded marriage may need to begin deep within the soul where our words originate. Have you examined your soul lately?

# 7

# The Anger

Wounded marriages usually contain a lot of anger—some verbal, some nonverbal. When you are hurt in a relationship, you are likely to feel that the pain is unjustified, and anger is a normal response. After all, why would someone who is supposed to love you cause so much pain in your life? Your spouse is supposed to be someone who protects, encourages, and supports you, not someone who inflicts so much heartache and pain.

It is very frustrating to be angry toward someone you once deeply loved, especially when the anger persists over a long period of time. We call this *unresolved anger*. It seems always to be there, even if just under the surface of day-to-day living.

*Melinda and Josh have been married almost eight years and now have two boys, ages five and seven. Melinda never finished college and has stayed home with the children since the birth of their first son. Josh is a nuclear scientist, highly trained for extremely technical*

48 Re-Igniting Love and Passion

*work. Moreover, he is a workaholic, putting in about twelve hours a day, six days a week. He is seldom home.*

*Melinda, a beautiful, sweet-spirited person, sat in my office with a slight smile on her face, appearing somewhat shy, even guilty for being there. However, her first words were: "I'm angry. I feel used. I feel alone. Josh is more in love with his work than he is with me."*

*Josh's typical day is like this: He gets up at 4:30 A.M. and is at work by 6:00 A.M. He returns home around 6:30 P.M., eats supper while watching television, plays with the boys for about an hour, and then falls in bed sound asleep by 8:30 P.M. Melinda is clearly left out of the picture. She is Josh's housekeeper, cook, baby-sitter, and occasional sexual outlet, week after week, month after month. She feels trapped in a dead-end marriage. After eight years, who wouldn't be angry with that kind of life?*

*Josh agreed to come for counseling. When confronted with the fact of Melinda's high level of hostility toward him, he simply responded, "I had no idea she was that angry!" Totally unaware of Melinda's anger, he sat shocked, stunned, and dismayed upon learning the truth. Fortunately, this revelation brought a serious commitment to change his lifestyle at home and at work.*

*Maria's anger was more severe. She came for counseling upon discovering her husband's infidelity. Ray had been clandestinely seeing his secretary in town and on business trips together. There is nothing like the pain of marital betrayal. Ray had stabbed Maria in the back. She wanted to hurt him in return. She wasn't sure what to do, but she wanted revenge.*

## Revenge or Punishment Theory

The *revenge or punishment theory* of anger, as applied to Maria's situation, is

| | |
|---|---|
| 1. I want something. | Maria wants a stable marriage with fidelity. |

# The Anger

| | |
|---|---|
| 2. You won't let me have it. | Ray's infidelity. |
| 3. That frustrates me. | Maria feels defeated in her aspirations for a happy marriage. |
| 4. People who frustrate me are bad. | Ray is now perceived not only as doing something morally wrong but also as a morally bad person. |
| 5. Bad persons should be punished. | Maria feels she has a right to retribution. |
| 6. Therefore, I will punish you with my anger. | Since physical punishment such as injuring or killing is frowned upon by our culture, Maria seeks to punish Ray with her anger. |

Without a doubt, anger is a normal first response for a woman who discovers that her husband is cheating on her. She would be considered strange or abnormal if it did not bother her. Ray's actions put Maria's marriage and personal well-being in jeopardy. Few would consider her wise to simply take it in stride and go on about her business. Ray's behavior severely wounded their marriage.

## Defense or Protection Theory

Another approach to understanding anger is the *defense or protection theory*. That is to say, anger is a means of defending yourself from a perceived threat. You use anger to protect yourself from some danger.

Maria certainly considered Ray's behavior as a threat to her marriage. She could choose anger as a way to protect a very important relationship. If she had chosen to divorce Ray, that would have been an expression of revenge or punishment. However, being counseled to fight for her marriage, she used anger to protect or defend herself from the threat of the other woman. This was a much more constructive use of anger than the revenge approach. She was no less angry, but she used anger to save her marriage. Therefore, she began by seeking counseling.

## It's Your Choice

To some degree, all emotions are chosen responses. It may not seem so at first, but a settled disposition of anger is chosen if it persists over enough time. The important thing to remember is that in choosing anger as a response, you also have to decide how to use it. What goals do you wish to accomplish with it? If you wish to save your wounded marriage, then you can choose to be motivated by anger to make the necessary changes. Constructive marriage counseling can assist you to discover those ways of thinking, acting, and feeling that need to be changed.

Either anger can motivate you to sink down in self-pity and resentment, seeking revenge, and trying to hurt your partner in order to punish him or her, or it can move you to pull up out of a routine, business-as-usual, somewhat dull relationship, take a good look at your situation, map out a strategy for change, and get to work on rekindling the flames of a dying romance.

*Maria was able to get Ray to come for counseling with her. Both discovered unmet needs in their relationship. However, Maria had*

# The Anger

*a low level of needs. She had been fairly satisfied with their marriage until she discovered Ray's unfaithfulness. Ray had a high level of needs. He had a strong need for sexual satisfaction, a strong desire to have Maria with him in his recreational outlets, a longing for admiration and affirmation, and a desire for Maria to be an attractive wife. Upon examination, Maria confessed that she flunked out on all of Ray's needs. Ray's secretary was an available and cooperative person to meet these needs.*

*Ray confessed that what he had done was morally and relationally wrong. He admitted that he should have sought counseling rather than another woman. He also admitted that he had not met Maria's needs for honesty and openness, family commitment, and affection to the degree that she desired.*

In this case, anger moved a wife to rebuild a broken relationship rather than to destroy it completely. Unfortunately, wounded marriages often move along over the years seething in unresolved anger. These are couples choosing to remain *hurt* rather than *helped*. If you are living in a wounded marriage, are you choosing to be hurt or helped?

If you can choose to be angry—and I believe it is a choice—then you can also choose how to use that anger. You do not have to be a victim of your emotions; you can use those emotions to become a victor.

Out-of-control anger, which can become hatred or rage, can be very destructive to a relationship. But anger under control can move you to change things that threaten the relationship. All of your emotions are God's gifts to *move* you to some kind of action. (Note the *mo* root form, from the Latin *movere*, meaning *to move*, underlying all such words as e*mo*tion, *mo*vement, *mo*tivation, e*mo*te, *mo*bility, *mo*tility, and *mo*ve.)

Anger can be an emotion to move you to change things: the unmet needs, the misunderstandings, the neglected important aspects, the priorities, the goals and objectives, the time schedules, the unkept promises of your relationship with your spouse. Anger can awaken you to the fact that this marriage is going down the drain and make you determined not to let that happen. Anger can spur you to do whatever is necessary to rebuild a neglected or damaged marital relationship.

Anger does not have to destroy a wounded marriage. It can be a powerful force in healing a wounded marriage. Anger can move you to

- forgive your spouse of whatever he or she has done to morally violate the relationship, or forgive him or her of the many neglectful inactions that communicated indifference or lack of love.
- begin consistently identifying and meeting the needs of your spouse (reread the needs list in chapter 4).
- work on improving your external, physical appearance. (Are you overweight, dowdy, drab, or unattractive?) Most men desire a wife who is sexually attractive at least some of the time. Likewise, most women prefer a husband who is good-looking, neat, and physically attractive.
- transform your attitudes, spirit, tone of voice, and manner of speaking. A loving wife knows how to turn her husband on with her voice: kind, sweet, attentive, considerate, empathetic, admiring, encouraging, affirming words. A loving husband can learn to do the same thing as he relates to his wife.

Let anger be your servant, not your master.

# 8

# The Fears

Anyone who lives in a wounded marriage understands the meaning of *fear*. No one who has stood at a wedding altar and pledged his or her love "till death do us part" wants to see that marriage fall apart. A lot of time, energy, and feelings have been invested in that relationship. Yet the wounds of a wounded marriage are symptomatic of potential marital failure, and the possibility of failure, separation, and eventually divorce is a frightening consideration.

## Fear of Failure

If the wounds never seem to heal, you begin to fear, "We're not going to make it." Fear of failure is itself a very painful experience, especially for Americans, whose culture teaches them that success in every aspect of life is the *summum bonum* of reality, and failure of any sort is the unpardonable sin.

We have all known people whose marriage has fallen apart and have observed their pain and sense of failure. Persons

53

in a wounded marriage are fearful that this could happen to them also, and this fear can have a paralyzing effect. You feel helpless to do anything about it, to make necessary changes, or to seek professional help.

You may be afraid to tell your friends that things are not well in your marriage. However, close friends probably already suspect that something is wrong; they simply haven't said anything. If you are active in a church, you certainly don't want the pastor to know your marriage is in trouble. God forbid! Not the pastor!

If you are active in some leadership or performance role in the church (e.g., deacon, elder, Sunday school teacher, youth leader, musician, committee chairman, trustee), you surely will not want to tell anyone in the congregation about your problems. The church wants you to be a marvelous, problem-free, even perfect example of Christian living. You know that a wounded marriage cannot measure up to such expectations, so you are afraid the truth will come out. You keep the problems to yourself, choosing instead to hurt in silence.

You are afraid to tell your children that their parents' marriage may be on the rocks, although more than likely they already know. However, if your children are grown and living in distant cities or if you are very good at hiding your problems, they may not know how serious the situation really is.

You may be afraid to tell your own parents that your marriage is about to end. You know that it will be extremely painful and disappointing for your parents to learn of this tragedy. Such fear adds to the pain of an already wounded relationship.

## Fear of the Unknown

Wounded marriages are also filled with fears regarding the unknown future. This is especially true for many women who are completely unprepared vocationally or financially to face a future alone. It isn't always easy or possible to re-

# The Fears 55

turn home to your parents. In addition, alimony and child support laws are not easily enforceable in many states.

*Sylvia and Mark had been married for eight-and-a-half years when Sylvia realized that their wounded marriage was likely to end in the near future. They had married right out of high school, so Sylvia had never gone on to college. She had gotten a job and helped put Mark through college. They now had one child, and another was on the way.*

*If she and Mark were to get a divorce, Sylvia wondered how she would survive financially. With no college education, no special training or marketable skills, and no job experience beyond minimum-wage work, Sylvia was frightened to death with the thought of making ends meet with two small children to feed and care for by herself. Her parents were divorced themselves, with neither one being in a position to help her.*

The fear of being alone, saddled with heavy responsibilities for your children, abandoned by your husband, with nowhere to go is not an uncommon fear of many women with little or no job experience who feel trapped in a wounded marriage.

## Fear of Losing the One You Love

Some women are fearful of losing their husband, whom they truly and honestly love, to another woman.

*Marge and Tom had been married almost twenty years when Marge began to realize over a period of time that Tom was not spending much time at home, especially evenings and weekends. When he was at home, he really seemed to be somewhere else. He had stopped showing Marge any special attention: no hugging, kissing, or other displays of affection. Their sex life was all but dead. They simply lived in the same house. The marriage had degenerated into being merely housemates who shared the same facilities but not their feelings or thoughts. There were no evenings out together for dinner or the theater as they had often done in the early years of marriage.*

*Then one evening Marge drove down to Tom's office to surprise him, to ask him to take her out for the evening. As she approached the office building, she saw Tom leaving with a woman Marge had never seen before. He had his arm around her waist. Tom didn't see Marge, but she was so shocked and hurt that she got back into her car and drove home.*

*Questions flooded her mind:*

*Who is this woman?*

*Is she the reason Tom often fails to come home after work?*

*Is Tom spending his weekends with her rather than doing what he claims ("just playing golf with some of the fellows")?*

*How could he do this to me?*

*Should I ask him about her?*

*Should I accuse him of possibly having an affair with this woman?*

*Am I just imagining all of this?*

*Should I just ignore what I saw and think only the best of him? (Maybe they were just innocently leaving the building together and are not really involved romantically.)*

*I've gained a lot of weight over the years and don't look as attractive as I used to. Has he just lost interest in me and is now attracted to a more beautiful and interesting woman?*

## Fear of Confrontation

All fears have a vivid imagination. This is especially so when coupled with the fear of confrontation about what is going on.

*Gary and Libby had been married for nine years when Gary began to notice that Libby was gradually distancing herself from him. Libby*

# The Fears                                           57

*was extremely beautiful, tall, and willowy, and she had an outgoing personality. She worked in a bank where she was very hopeful of promotions that would take her to the top ranks.*

*Gary knew that some of Libby's superiors were men of few scruples regarding another man's wife. Libby began to work late at the bank and to take business trips with her associates. Gary's own job situation was somewhat stagnant with his promotion possibilities having hit a ceiling. Libby was already making more money than he and stood to do even better if she pleased her superiors. Gary began to realize that his chances of being dumped by Libby were increasing. The bank president was especially attentive to her. Gary's fears of losing Libby were growing. Such fears can quickly become panic.*

## Use Your Fear

How can a wounded marriage handle fear constructively? Well, the choice is yours. Either you can choose to allow such fears to paralyze you into inaction or even stupid actions (which are really reactions), or you can choose to take charge of your fears and utilize them to motivate you to make some necessary, constructive changes.

I assume you would prefer to do the latter or you wouldn't be reading this book. The apostle Paul reminded his young friend Timothy that "God did not give us a spirit of timidity [fear, KJV; cowardice, NRSV], but a spirit of power, of love and of self-discipline" (2 Tim. 1:7). Countless times, the Bible calls upon believers to realize that since we are always in the presence of God, we are able to "fear not."

Fear is a natural emotion—one of God's gifts to warn us of impending danger. But God wants to replace our fears with trust and reason (common sense). Yet fear also has value if you allow the Lord to direct your steps. If yours is a wounded marriage, fear can motivate you to

- recognize that a problem exists. There is real or potential danger that your marriage may be in serious trouble.
- admit to yourself that you have probably contributed to your marriage's problems in a number of ways. Identify those contributions specifically. Yes, your spouse has contributed to these problems also, but you cannot do anything about that now. You can deal only with your own contributions.
- determine now to seek professional help—a qualified and competent professional counselor. You may not like what you will learn in counseling, but it's an important place to start.
- join and faithfully participate in a small support group for persons in wounded marriages. If you cannot find one, ask your pastor or other church staff members to start and lead one. If that is not possible, then ask your professional counselor to assist you in locating one in your city or community.
- determine now to set about to grow spiritually in your relationship with God. He will be your ultimate source for help and direction. Work on changing yourself, becoming a strong and faithful Christian. What areas of your personality and character need radical alteration? Focus on making those changes. A new and better situation is possible only if you become a new and qualitatively different (better) person. Counsel with your pastor about how this can be done. If he is not interested or does not understand what you are talking about, then find another pastor who is interested in your spiritual growth and who is sensitive to the needs of a wounded marriage.

# 9

## The Tears

Most people who find themselves living in a wounded marriage have shed their share of tears. They have fallen asleep many a night on a tear-soaked pillow. They cannot understand what has happened to a relationship that was so wonderful and ecstatic at first. The expectations that were brought into the marriage have all been shattered by confusing reality.

The hopes, dreams, and aspirations of what was once a very tender and affectionate coupling have now been lost, and loss results in grief, and grief often expresses itself in tears. But tears are God's gift to the grieving that allow pent-up emotions to be openly expressed in what can prove to be a constructive outlet.

The alternative is to repress these feelings of loss and grief over a marriage that has gone sour. Persistent repression can be very detrimental to your mental, emotional, and physical health. An ongoing sense of loss of something once treasured can in time weaken your immune system or cause clinical depression.

Tears, on the other hand, can function as a healthy release of your feelings of sorrow and sadness. This can give you a reprieve from the pain long enough to get back in control of your life and begin making some new and constructive decisions about your relationship.

*I recall Bob and Jennifer's crumbling marriage. Bob was a big, muscular, macho man. He told me that he could count on the fingers of one hand the number of times he had cried in his thirty-six years. He grew up in a typical American home where he was taught both directly and indirectly that "boys aren't supposed to cry"—it was a sign of weakness. Externally strong and tough, Bob had been a very good football and baseball player in college. Until now, he allowed only the tough guy to come through.*

*However, when Jennifer ran off with another man and left Bob with their three children, the sadness and grief were too much even for big Bob. His tears, shed first in my office while telling me about what had happened, were a painful acknowledgment of his inability to control everything that went on around him. Nothing he could say or do was going to bring Jennifer back, he reasoned. He felt like he was in an automobile that was careening over a cliff, and there was absolutely nothing he could do to stop it from crashing at the bottom. This was his first introduction to his limited humanity.*

*Tears often flowed after Bob retired to his bedroom at night, having put the kids to bed as he tried to maintain some degree of normalcy for them. After ten years of marriage to Jennifer, her abandonment of him and the children left Bob numb, confused, sad, and angry.*

*At first his sorrow was for himself; after all, he was Jennifer's husband, the father of her children. But as the weeks went by, Bob's sadness extended to his children and eventually to his parents as well as Jennifer's parents. The entire family was in a state of grief worse than a death. There was no body to bury, no way to put this loss behind them. Bob, the children, and both sets of parents began to discover ways to care for each other with compassion in the context of a wounded and dying marriage.*

# The Tears

*Bob's tears of grief brought out an inner self he never knew existed. This was a person who could be soft with compassion and understanding. He was learning that this was not a time to be tough, hard, distant, and unapproachable. The other members of the family needed him now more than ever before. Tears that could have been merely self-pity became tears of empathy for the children and self-examination for himself. Where had he gone wrong? Where had he failed Jennifer? What was there about him that drove her into another man's arms? These and similar questions were washed through his mind by the tears.*

*A few months later I learned that Jennifer had been shedding her share of tears as well, but hers were tears of guilt and shame. A typical American mother cannot abandon her children and not feel some guilt, some regret, some shame. She later told me that she left Bob primarily because she felt like she could never get close to him. His tough exterior seemed impenetrable. There was no authentic intimacy between them.*

*The other man came along and seemingly offered her all that she had hoped for in Bob but never got. However, it didn't take long for Jennifer to discover that her feelings for the other man were based on fantasy rather than reality. The other man turned out to be slick, manipulative, and disgustingly selfish. It gradually dawned on Jennifer that all this other man really wanted was sex and the income from her job. He was a smooth talker, and she fell for his every word.*

*In a few months Jennifer was crying herself to sleep at night wondering how she could have been so stupid and, yes, immoral. Her tears of guilt and shame soon turned into tears of remorse and repentance. She called me one day to ask if I would try to set up some reconciliation counseling between herself and Bob. I was convinced that she was sincere. When I called Bob to tell him what was going on with Jennifer, he was naturally skeptical and even cynical to some degree.*

*However, this was a new Bob, broken by what had happened, and I was able to persuade him to give Jennifer a chance. She had left the man she ran off with and was trying to make an honest comeback.*

62  Re-Igniting Love and Passion

*Counseling with her individually, I was able to guide her in putting the broken pieces of her life back together, even though it was slow and painful. The guilt and shame had shattered her self-image; her self-esteem was on the floor. But with God's help, she was inching her way back.*

*I will never forget the first session when Bob and Jennifer came for counseling together. There were a lot of tears shed during that session. For Bob there were tears of anger mingled with forgiveness. For Jennifer there were tears of confession and repentance. Together, before the session ended, there were many tears of reconciliation.*

*This was just the beginning of their getting back together again. Many difficult counseling sessions followed, both individually and as a couple. There was a lot of unfinished business to resolve and many wounds to heal. Bob had to learn how to open up and allow himself to be vulnerable, intimate, and close in his relationship with Jennifer, and she had to learn how to be patient, kind, and affectionate. Both had to learn how to meet each other's needs, how to complement each other emotionally and relationally, while giving each other some private space at the same time.*

*Jennifer's tears of confession and repentance had to be shed also in front of her three children who, although very confused as to why she would leave them, were still glad to have her back. The children shed their share of tears also, and they engaged in several weeks of counseling to work through their feelings regarding their mother's abandonment. In many wounded marriages the children feel that the problems were somehow their fault, and those feelings of self-blame are not easy to overcome and work through.*

*In Bob and Jennifer's case, the tears became the means for eventual healing and restoration. They could have been tears of anger, resentment, and bitterness with no hope of recovery or reconciliation. What made the difference? The only answer I can honestly suggest is the grace of God. You see, this was a Christian marriage and family, at least to some degree. They were not bereft or ignorant of certain divine resources. In their pain they cried out to God the only way they knew how, and he heard their cry; he saw*

# The Tears 63

*their tears. God went to work when the tears of Bob and Jennifer and the children opened their hearts to his special intervention.*

I am reminded of the story in John's Gospel, chapter 11. There had been a serious loss: Mary and Martha's brother, Lazarus, had died. They sent for Jesus. When Jesus arrived, he assessed the situation and identified with their grief, and verse 35 (the shortest in the Bible) simply says, "Jesus wept." But then Jesus moved quickly to redemptive action: He went to the tomb of Lazarus, called out his name, and raised him back to life.

Our tears mingled with Jesus' tears can restore a wounded and dying marriage. Invite Jesus into your situation and see what he can do. Remember, he is in the resurrection business.

# 10

# The Denials

Persons in wounded marriages spend a lot of time in denial. It is difficult to admit this kind of pain to yourself or to others. You may feel like running away when

- your love for each other has grown cold or mechanical.
- you realize that the high expectations of the early days of your marriage will never be reached.
- the conflict between you continues with heated words or has settled into quiet and controlled anger.
- your sex life is no longer enjoyable or lovingly intimate.
- the tears continue to flow most nights before you drop off into a restless and disturbing sleep.

One way some people run away is through denial.

Psychologically, denial is an unconscious defense mechanism of ignoring the existence of painful realities. Denial is largely a subconscious technique that enables you to escape from intolerable thoughts, wishes, actions, feelings, or

65

events as well as the extremely uncomfortable anxiety that they produce. Denial is not usually intentional lying or malingering, nor is it a deliberate repudiation or dismissal of the negative situation or feelings. You may simply fail to consciously perceive that they exist.

There are different forms or expressions of denial. You may become totally unaware that you have strong feelings of hostility toward your spouse or that your spouse is often cruel, insensitive, or abusive. You may fail to see your spouse's mistreatment of you although it is quite obvious to everyone else. You may lose your sense of reality and feel, "this isn't happening to me."

Sometimes defensive denial takes the form of cheerful though shallow unconcern over what is happening in the relationship. In other cases the harsh facts of the marriage cannot be faced and dealt with, and so denial results.

Other forms of denial are not subconscious. If pressed with the truth about a bad marriage, you may admit that you have learned to survive by screening out the unpleasant aspects and disagreeable realities of the relationship. You put off making decisions that need to be made. You ignore problems you do not wish to solve. You suddenly become intensely preoccupied when certain disagreeable issues arise. Through these techniques of denial, you do not deny the reality of problems, but you refuse to give them your best and undivided attention.

Denial may sometimes help to shelter you from stress and painful anxiety or give you time for making thoughtful decisions. As a regular pattern of action, however, denial will ultimately interfere with your adjustment since it is a way of dodging problems and hardships instead of facing them with courage, thought, wisdom, and counsel on the way toward arriving at constructive solutions.

It is also important to realize that persons in a wounded marriage are experiencing grief to a great extent, and denial is one of the recognized stages of grief. Whether gradually

# The Denials

or suddenly, a spouse in a wounded marriage will eventually realize that this marriage is not a happy one, that there are more negatives than positives, and that the couple simply might not be able to work out this incompatible situation into a satisfactory solution. Consequently, there comes an inevitable sense of loss very similar to a death, except here there is no body to bury. You feel that you have lost your marriage; maybe you even feel that the marriage is dead. Given what you originally thought it would be—grand and glorious—the hard reality of a relationship gone sour floods you with an awesome sense of sadness. The first response to such grief is often a feeling of shock and denial.

I have observed that a common denial technique in wounded marriages is to retreat into various forms of diversionary activity, naively hoping that the problem or conflict will go away in time. This is fantasy, a form of infantile reasoning: "I will put my head into the sand of some trivial diversion (that has nothing to do with the marriage), and when I come up for air, the problem will no longer exist."

*Cybil had great difficulty being sexually affectionate with her husband, Art; she was never very demonstrative. Moreover, she knew that if she went to bed by 10:00 P.M., it would trigger Art into thinking about having sexual relations, something she really did not care much about. So Cybil chose to stay up as late as possible so that Art would be too sleepy and tired to have sex. Her diversionary activity was either to watch late movies on television or to read a book in the den.*

*At other times, Cybil would engage in such diversionary actions as sewing, gardening, or attending weeknight church meetings—things in which Art was not particularly interested. The problem wasn't that Art wanted only sex from Cybil. He merely wanted intimacy, open affection, and expressed affirmation from the woman he thought he loved and whom he thought loved him. Cybil's attitude toward Art and his needs was very simple: "When I am intimate and sexual, I am being used, and that makes me feel very cheap."*

*Counseling revealed that Cybil's attitude had developed in early childhood. Cybil's mother had taught her lesson well: "All men want is sex. They don't care a thing about you as a person. In the end you will end up being a doormat; yes, even when you are a married woman." Cybil's mother had learned this directly from Cybil's father and indirectly from all the other men in her extended family.*

*In the meantime, Art's needs for affection and affirmation went largely unmet. As the months passed, he began to feel that Cybil really did not love him, since she tended to avoid him in the area of intimacy. He felt cheated and deprived. The relationship began to falter, and Cybil knew it. But instead of facing the problem, she chose to deny it by engaging in all sorts of diversionary busyness that would keep her mind off of Art's unhappiness and disappointment with her. This would also keep her mind off of her own guilt-ridden resistance to intimacy.*

*Cybil was basically a very self-centered person who had no idea what her husband's psychological and relational needs were. She never really thought about the fact that a married man has needs that only his wife can or should meet. On the other hand, Art had no idea why Cybil was so self-contained, independent, self-satisfied, aloof, and distant, even though arguments were a common pattern of relating in their marriage.*

*Art eventually began to deny the pain in his marriage by reaching out in overly friendly ways to certain female clients and associates in his business. His denial was to get lost and involved in other types of relationships. Naturally, this made him quite vulnerable to becoming unfaithful to Cybil. After long periods of no requests for sex by Art, Cybil eventually became suspicious that he might be having an affair. Even though she was living in much denial regarding an unhappy marriage, Cybil really didn't want to see her marriage fall apart by Art running off with another woman.*

*The mutual denial of Cybil and Art almost cost them their marriage. They came to me for counseling and began the long road back to learning to meet each other's needs. Their initial step toward recovery was to pull out of the tailspin of denial, to face up to the realities of the relationship, and to recognize that one of the main*

# The Denials

*reasons they got married in the first place was to complement each other in a sacred oneness and to blend together in an enjoyable relationship of mutual affirmation and encouragement.*

*Art and Cybil had a lot of grief work to do in several weeks of counseling. After working through the denial stage of a dead marriage, they had to work through considerable anger and guilt regarding the way they had treated each other. They also had to work through a sense of hopelessness and helplessness about future prospects for recovery.*

*Then Art and Cybil moved through the stage of bargaining with each other: If you do this, then I'll do that; I'll try to be a better spouse if you will; etc. Such conditional relating runs contrary to that which makes for a successful marriage: unconditional love. Finally, they reached the stage of unconditional acceptance—accepting each other "warts and all." Neither will ever be perfect, but two people can learn to accept each other's imperfections and move on from there to acknowledge that each possesses strengths and good points that attracted them to each other in the beginning.*

If you are in a wounded marriage, you need to carefully determine whether you are in one of these forms of denial. You may need to accept the reality of grief over a marriage that is dead or dying. You may need to learn how to move through the various stages of grief toward acceptance and recommitment to a resurrection of the relationship.

Resurrection? Yes, resurrection! "But," you may say, "I thought only God could do that." That's right. Only God, but he *can* do it! Yet a vital part of resurrection is the willingness to crawl out of the tomb of denial. Remember Lazarus (read John 11:1–44).

# 11

# The Bedroom

Wounded marriages suffer some of their greatest injuries in the bedroom. The bedroom represents the full range of marital intimacy, but sleeping together certainly focuses upon the sexual life of a married couple. Sex is not everything in a marriage, but it obviously functions as a relational thermometer for a husband and wife.

Usually sex is not the *cause* of marital conflict, rather it is "the nail on which much marital conflict hangs." Potential areas of conflict include:

- incompatible personalities of the couple
- conflicts rooted in the job situation
- financial stress (too many debts, not enough money)
- differences over child-rearing techniques
- problems with in-laws or other relatives
- religious differences
- family disagreements (he wants to take a vacation, while she wants to stay home)
- differences over major purchases (a car, a house, a farm, a business, etc.)

When these nonsexual conflicts get out of hand and are seemingly unresolvable and ongoing, the hostile atmosphere that often results can seep its way into the bedroom at night and negatively affect the couple's sexual behavior. It is next to impossible to make love enjoyably and intimately when these types of conflict lurk in the back of your mind.

## Unfinished Business

Another culprit in the marital bedroom is what is commonly called *unfinished business* from childhood. Amy and Don's wounded marriage is a good example.

*Amy had been reared in a home where her father was often absent, and when he was there, he was cold and distant. Amy commented: "I think my father loved me, but he rarely if ever showed it." She was never invited to sit on his lap; he never read to her or sang to her. They never went for walks together. They never played games together.*

*Yet Amy desperately wanted a warm and loving relationship with her father. In a sense, when she married Don, Amy was hoping that Don would be that kind of father to her. Now as a married woman, Amy expected that sex with Don would give her that feeling of warmth and acceptance.*

*However, Don had his own unfinished business from childhood to deal with. Don's mother was very controlling and domineering. Her love for Don was almost smothering in that she manipulated and used him for her own purposes. Don deeply resented this overbearing control. When he married Amy, he was hoping that she would be the kind of woman who would give him his freedom and who would not try to dominate him.*

*So as it turned out, Don was not able to be the father figure Amy had longed for, and Amy could not be the kind of mother figure Don needed. Therefore, in the bedroom Don needed to control Amy (by being the dominant sexual partner), while Amy needed a sensitive, warm, and*

# The Bedroom

*understanding partner. Consequently, their sex life was anything but complementary. Neither got what they were expecting or desiring in bed.*

*Amy interpreted Don's sexual behavior as aloof, impersonal, and insensitive—the personality attributes of her father. When Don saw or thought of Amy in bed, he was subconsciously reminded of his mother. That is, Don was fearful that Amy would be just like his mother in efforts to control and manipulate him. The unfinished business of both childhoods continued to plague Don and Amy into their adult years. Their bedroom seemed to be where this incongruity most often came to a head.*

*The sex life of Don and Amy proved to be symptomatic of deeper and more long-standing problems in their personal and family backgrounds. Both made the mistake of expecting their chosen spouse to somehow resolve the unfinished business of their childhood.*

The truth of the matter is that there is only one person who can deal with and work toward the resolution of your unfinished business out of the past, and that person is yourself. It is unfair to expect your spouse to do for you what only you can do for yourself.

If the problems from your childhood are beyond your ability to understand and resolve, then get some competent help from a qualified counselor or therapist. Your marriage needs to be free from the harassment of an emotionally handicapped inner child of the past. Your marriage does not need the excess baggage of unmet needs from your childhood.

## Sexual Abuse

Another couple I worked with represent another form of woundedness that is brought out in the marital bedroom.

*Alice had been sexually abused the first time when she was only five years old, and a similar form of abuse happened a few times over the next six years. The abuse was carried out by peers of her brother, while her older brother stood by and watched. At age twenty-four, she told of these events for the first time.*

*Alice recalled the abuse with considerable disgust, not only because of what those boys did, but also because her brother allowed it and did nothing to prevent it. Her first conclusion regarding sex and sexuality was: "This is the way males treat females. They are all potentially abusive, and I'm not going to let it happen to me again."*

*But at sixteen, lonely and hurting from the painful and frightening divorce of her parents, Alice reached out to take whatever love she could find. Having never felt fully loved by anyone in her family, she craved whatever affection was available. A high-school boyfriend filled that gap. Not understanding the biological process of how one gets pregnant, Alice was overwhelmed by this seventeen-year-old boy's physical affection and was soon inflicted with an unwanted pregnancy. The eventual abandonment by the child's father only confirmed Alice's earlier conclusion about males.*

*At age twenty-three, Alice and her child found themselves in need of protection and care. So she married Rob, who at age twenty-seven offered her stability and security—the two things she felt she needed most at that time.*

*Rob's steady interest in sex would be considered normal for a male his age, and Alice was very sexually attractive. But Rob was not prepared to deal with all of Alice's sexual hang-ups. When Rob tried to make love to her, Alice would conjure up in her mind all of the negative images of sexual abuse and an unwanted pregnancy. In the early days of their marriage, Alice admitted that she just gritted her teeth and tolerated sex. Rob felt rebuffed to some degree and didn't understand why.*

*After a year of marriage, the scene at bedtime became a most unpleasant experience for both of them. Alice began to make excuses for not having sexual relations. Frequency diminished to about once a month. With Rob threatening divorce, Alice finally sought counseling to find some reasonable solutions. Tracing back her feelings to those earlier experiences of sexual abuse helped her immensely in understanding why she felt the way she did. Behind*

# The Bedroom

*their bedroom difficulties were deeper injuries out of the past that needed to be healed. Resolution was a long time in coming, but it came.*

## Physical Problems

*Jerold and Louise almost divorced because of bedroom trauma but for a different reason. Jerold was one of my seminary students who heard a noted Christian gynecologist whom I had invited to speak on various medical ethical issues. Something the doctor said in his lecture about the sexual aspects of marriage later brought Jerold to my office.*

*I could tell that he was extremely hesitant to tell me what the problem was. Finally, Jerold blurted it out: His wife refused to have sex with him because she claimed it was all very painful—too painful to tolerate. The amazing thing about this was that Louise had been to four different doctors, and each one, too busy to give her a careful exam, concluded that her problem was simply psychological. None gave a satisfactory explanation.*

*I recommended that Jerold take his wife to see my gynecologist friend who had lectured in class. This particular doctor had been a great help to my own wife with a very serious problem, the cause of which other gynecologists had overlooked. Jerold took the doctor's phone number and said he would make an appointment for Louise.*

*Jerold's visit to my office was at the end of the spring semester, and I did not see them during the summer months. But at the beginning of the fall semester, Jerold came bouncing into my office, grabbed me, gave me a big hug, and exclaimed, "You saved my marriage!" After reminding me of his request for help three months earlier, he told me that my doctor friend examined his wife and found that there was a physical obstruction at the entrance of the vagina (similar to but different from her original hymen). A minor surgical procedure removed the obstruction, and in a short time they were able to have painless sexual relations for the first time. Jerold was indeed one happy husband.*

I wish that every bedroom marriage problem could be solved that easily. But it does illustrate that some problems are physical and need competent and careful medical attention.

The writer to the Hebrews offered these practical words: "Marriage should be honored by all, and the marriage bed kept pure, for God will judge the adulterer and all the sexually immoral" (Heb. 13:4). The marriage bed needs not only to be kept pure from infidelity but also unobstructed by either physical or psychological impairments, because many good marriages can either be made or undone in the bedroom. Likewise, the healing of many wounded marriages can often begin in the bedroom. God wants your bedroom to be a happy place, full of pleasure, rest, and even laughter.

# 12

## The Children

The Bible teaches that children are a blessing from God (see Pss. 37:26; 127:3–5 NRSV), but wounded marriages have some of their greatest conflicts over differences of opinion regarding the children.

### Child-Rearing Disagreements

Spouses who grew up in families with significantly different philosophies of child-rearing may find it difficult to resolve those differences because people tend to raise their children as they were raised. If the husband grew up in a family where his parents practiced a very strict approach in discipline and the wife was raised in a family that followed a rather permissive approach, then these two opposed approaches are bound to create conflict in the rearing of their own children.

*Kevin's parents were very strict, even using physical forms of punishment. As Kevin often said, "When I got out of line, my dad*

77

*would whomp me a good one with his belt, and it worked with me. So why not deal with my own kids the same way? It ought to work with them too."*

*However, Marla was raised by parents who used rational approaches, depending on calm, verbal directions and explanations rather than spanking or threats. Marla's parents followed an approach similar to that of Rudolf Dreikurs, who advocated the use of "natural and logical consequences" for discipline rather than punishment.[13] Kevin argued that Marla's approach was soft and permissive and would produce uncontrolled kids, while Marla believed that Kevin's approach was harsh and, in the long run, would do more harm than good.*

*These two approaches clashed in Kevin and Marla's marriage and created considerable confusion and frustration for their children. In their confusion, and somewhat as a defense mechanism, Marla and Kevin's children would often subconsciously pit each parent against the other, creating further conflict.*

*Their opposing parenting skills put unusual strain on Marla and Kevin's marriage. Neither parent was willing to give in to the other's way of discipline, each thinking the other was wrong. Conflict escalated, and in time, the marriage became wounded.*

## The Blame Game

Children can also play another role in a wounded marriage: Morally and spiritually wayward children can inflict considerable damage on their parents' marriage. Especially Christian parents, who have honestly tried to raise their children in the atmosphere of a Christian home but have had at least one child reject the morality and faith of their home, can end up being wounded parents who turn on each other. Each blames the other for why a child went astray, and they can easily end up with a wounded marriage.[14]

# The Children

Some marriages are more fragile than others, and children usually do not realize that their rebellious behavior can adversely affect their parents' marriage.

*Sam and Nora were the parents of three children. The oldest, an unmarried daughter, got pregnant in her late teens. The baby's father, also in his late teens, had no intentions of marrying their daughter. As devout Christians and very active in their church, Sam and Nora were facing a major crisis.*

*Sam was a very busy businessman who often traveled out of town and was away from the family for several days at a time. Nora worked for a real estate firm and was quite good at selling, but her work kept her away from home a lot. So when their daughter got pregnant, Sam and Nora blamed each other for what had happened. Each accused the other: "If you had been home more often, if you had not been so consumed in your work, if you had given that girl more attention, . . ."*

*Each played "the blame game,"[15] which never goes anywhere and in which there are no winners, only losers. Consequently, their marriage suffered. Neither assumed any responsibility for what had happened—not that it was necessarily the fault of either of them. Each simply laid the blame for this embarrassing situation at the feet of the other. They failed to see that they needed to be supportive of each other and especially of their daughter, who was the most immediate victim of her own bad judgment. Turning on each other merely aggravated the situation and made the predicament worse.*

## Physical or Psychological Needs

Children can also be the precipitating cause of a wounded marriage when there are medical, physiological, or psychiatric complications with the children, especially if the marriage relationship is not strong to begin with. Instances where a child has Down's syndrome, severe asthma, A.D.D.

# 80 Re-Igniting Love and Passion

(attention deficit disorder), brain damage (whatever the initial cause), deafness, blindness, or various mental disorders (schizophrenia, manic-depressive, psychotic tendencies, or others) can place considerable long-term strain on the parents' marriage.

*Jane and Terry had two sons, Buz (age seven) and Blake (age five) when they came for counseling. Buz seemed normal in all of his physical and mental functions. However, Blake's behavior was quite problematic: He was a whiner, hyperactive, loud, disruptive in groups, extremely nervous, and seldom able to sit still for very long. He also cried a lot and had a very short attention span. Blake demanded all of his parents' attention—so much so that poor Buz was sorely neglected most of the time.*

*Totally perplexed about what to do, Jane and Terry had reached a point of utter frustration. Jane seemed to be somewhat of a nervous, high-strung person herself. She could become very emotional if she felt that Blake was being criticized by his teachers in kindergarten or Sunday school. Since Blake had almost died shortly after childbirth, Jane tended to be overprotective of him. Both parents largely avoided disciplinary controls on Blake until his behavior would get completely out-of-hand, especially in public.*

*I referred this couple to a child psychiatrist, since the situation was obviously beyond my counseling skills. When the psychiatrist diagnosed Blake with attention deficit disorder, I was not surprised. With medication and some parenting skills guidance, the psychiatrist was able to stabilize Blake's behavior toward a more normal pattern.*

*If Jane and Terry had not gotten professional help for this special problem, I feel fairly certain that their marriage would have eventually collapsed. They were already emotionally strained to the limits when they came to see me. Each had begun to harshly blame the other for Blake's uncontrollable actions, when, in fact, the root of the problem was the fault of neither of them.*

# The Children

81

## Childlessness

Another situation where the subject of children can be a major catalyst for a wounded marriage is when one spouse wants to have children and the other does not. I have never understood why such couples did not discuss and settle this matter *before* they got married. But I have had married women cry their hearts out in my office because after a year or more of marriage, they found out that their husband did not really want children. I had one wife tell me that her husband had threatened to leave her if she got pregnant! Another husband had been telling his wife for six years, "Not now, maybe later." (See Marsha and Lynn's story in chapter 6.)

The only way I have found to help such couples is to probe for the deeper psychological reasons why a spouse does not want children (other than just not liking or wanting kids). There is usually a reason rooted deep in the past that has never been discussed between the couple. Until this reason can be identified and understood, there is not much that can be done to heal the hurt of a disappointed spouse who wants a child.

Since between 10 to 15 percent of married couples are unable to have children, it would be expected that some marriages experience considerable strain over their childlessness, especially when both desperately want a child of their own. Some of these couples go to great expense working with fertility specialists for several years. Recent medical technology has made it possible for some couples to eventually succeed in having a child, but this does not always work. After spending thousands of dollars, some couples in dire frustration over the failure to get pregnant sometimes turn on and wound each other.

It is sad that some of these childless couples are unwilling to go the adoption route when there are children available to be adopted. Adoption can be expensive also, but it is an option that has been joyfully experienced by many couples.

## A Strong Marriage Makes Better Parents

Marriage and parenting can be both enjoyable and difficult. They both call for mature and stable adults who have the mental, emotional, and spiritual strength to succeed. Children present a particular challenge to parents to be strong in both love and understanding. Every couple should discuss thoroughly each individual's values regarding family life *before* they get married. Know what you are getting into. Before children are conceived and brought into the world, make sure your marriage is strong and mature. After all, the best thing any couple can give their children is a father and mother who love each other and have a good marriage.

A pastor friend once told me of a couple in his church where the father was a traveling salesman who was gone from home each week, Monday through Friday. He tried to give his best to his wife and three grade-school sons on the weekends.

One Tuesday evening after the boys had come home from school, the mother had set the supper table. The oldest son came into the dining room and noticed that the meal consisted of warmed up leftovers from Sunday. He said, "Mama, why is it that when Daddy's home you fix the best meals in town, but when Daddy's gone, you fix us *this?*" pointing in disgust to the leftovers.

The mother responded with the wisdom of Solomon, "Son, it's like this: Your father and I have a permanent commitment; you kids are just passing through."

A wise mother indeed! This was no put-down of her kids. She was saying to her children that in a day of many single-parent homes and failing marriages, the one thing they could count on was the strong marriage of their parents. What a gift to her children!

# 13

## The Relatives

A marriage can suffer a variety of wounds over conflicts regarding the couple's relatives. The proverbial mother-in-law, however, is not the only potential culprit. The conflict can focus upon *any* relative who seeks to interfere and is allowed to disrupt the couple's marriage. It just *seems* like the mother-in-law (either one of the mothers) is often the major problem in a young couple's efforts to have a good marriage.

## Interfering Mothers

During my high-school and college days, I can recall several couples I knew who divorced over conflicts precipitated by his or her mother. I wondered then: Why would her mother (or his mother) want to break up the marriage? I had no answer then, but age, experience, and maturity helped me find some possible explanations for such perplexing questions.

84 Re-Igniting Love and Passion

You would be hard-pressed to find a relative who honestly believes that he or she is intentionally interfering with someone's marriage. Interfering relatives are usually blind to what they are doing. They would naturally consider any critical comments as well intentioned, regardless of the fallout.

*José and Bonita had been married for only a few weeks when Bonita was visiting with her mother one day. They were in the kitchen preparing the evening meal. José was not in the house at the time. Bonita's mother, Carmen, took this opportunity to complain to her daughter about some of José's bad habits. Bonita could have taken her mother's criticisms seriously enough that she might have begun deeply questioning her choice of José as her husband, but Bonita was smarter than that.*

*After a few minutes of hearing Carmen's undermining of José, Bonita stopped her mother and said, "Mother, you are talking about my husband. I don't like for you to do that. I don't want to ever hear you talk that way again. Do I make myself clear?" Carmen sheepishly responded, "Well, I was just trying to help." Help?*

*Carmen's problem was that she had always seen herself as mother, and she believed mothers should give advice, be in charge of the children, and protect them from harm. Bonita's recent marriage to José meant to Carmen that she might lose her role of mother. It never occurred to her that she had another role that she needed to focus on: wife to her own husband, Ramon.*

*Carmen could not accept the fact that her daughter was now a grown, married woman. For many years into Bonita's adult life Carmen often said, "You will always be my little girl." Carmen would never entertain the thought that this was very demeaning to Bonita, who did not want to be anyone's "little girl" any longer.*

Some mothers simply cannot give up their children to adult life and responsibility. They seek to hang onto the past, and this can easily become serious interference in the children's marriages. The only way to deal with this is for the children to remind their parents that they are adults and ask

# The Relatives 85

them to stop such interferences, just as Bonita did with her mother. Relatives can become a threat to your marriage only if you allow them to interfere.

A part of the problem is that most young adult children naturally still love and respect their parents. They appreciate what their parents have done for them through the years. This is doubly true if the parents have given considerable monetary assistance to help the kids to get off to a good start in the marriage. Sometimes this kind of money has strings attached: "Since we gave you this money (and may still be doing so), then we reserve the right to give you our advice." Wise adult married children will not accept anyone's gifts of money if there are unacceptable strings attached.

## Controlling Fathers

Some fathers may also be inclined to want to control their children after they get married. Common advice is: "Stay in school and get a good education so you can make a decent living. Don't get pregnant just yet. Delay starting your family until you can afford to raise children. Let us help you get on your feet." This may be good advice, but it is unwise to allow someone else to make your decisions for you.

Other fathers try to control a son (or son-in-law) by trying to pull him into the family business when the young husband prefers to go his own way. If the son balks, the father may try to lay a guilt trip on him by saying, "But I built up this business just for you!" If you do decide to go into business with him, let it be your decision, not his.

Some fathers will say to their daughters: "If he is ever unkind to you, if the marriage becomes difficult, if you realize you made a mistake, if you are ever unhappy, then, honey, just come on back home. We are still your parents, and we still love you and will take you back." Where such advice is given, the chances of a divorce taking place are greatly increased, because every marriage will experience its tough times calling for difficult adjustments. Providing an easy escape hatch makes it much more likely that it will be used.

Much wiser and loving was the father who said to his daughter on her wedding day: "Honey, we are so happy you have found your true love and are getting married. Give it your best and work hard to make it succeed. Your mother and I want you to know that we will be praying for you both to have a good marriage, and when you have those inevitable difficult days, please don't run away from them. Although we will always love you, you are now becoming his wife, and your new role takes priority over all other relationships. Make your marriage work; trust the Lord, and he will help you. Don't run from difficulty. Stay and work it out. As the years go by, you will be glad you did."

An exception to the above would be if there is severe physical or emotional abuse. In such cases, it is appropriate for relatives to intervene to protect the abused and seek help for the abuser. If the husband refuses to get professional counseling for his abuse problem, then the wife needs to report her husband to the appropriate law enforcement agency. This can be an emotionally devastating experience, and the abused wife will need to be able to rely on the love and support of her relatives.

## Clashing Value Systems

Some marriages become wounded by sharp differences of opinion over the clashing value systems of the families from which each spouse comes.

*Paul and Connie came from quite different family backgrounds regarding finances. Simply put, Paul's parents were savers, while*

*Connie's parents were spenders. Paul's parents kept insisting that they save, save, save, probably because they remembered the tough times they had when they started out. Connie's parents urged them to spend, spend, spend, probably to make sure they "keep up with the Joneses."*

*Since Connie's parents never taught her the value of a dollar, Paul was miffed when Connie would follow her mother's urging to go out and buy this or that whether they had the money or not. No wonder the marriage was one long battle over money. Again, parental messages kept interfering. Paul and Connie had to work out a compromise of their own that they could live with: Paul needed to loosen up, while Connie needed to tighten up regarding their spending habits.*

## Ending the Interference

Grandparents, brothers and sisters, aunts and uncles, and even cousins can also be the focus of conflict for wounded marriages. So what do you do? You can love and respect your relatives without allowing them to overly influence you. You have to decide whether or not you are going to function as a mature adult, capable of making your own decisions.

One thing a couple can learn to do with regard to the attempts of relatives to unduly influence or control them: Learn to say "no." You don't need to argue with them. You don't need to be defensive with them in the face of their advice. If going against their efforts to influence you will cause them to no longer love you, then recognize that such love is actually conditional love, and Christians, of all people, should know that that's not the kind of love that families should practice. Such relatives may need a few gentle lectures on the nature of unconditional love.

It is important to recognize that when relatives contribute to the wounding of a marriage, it is usually because they were allowed to do so. This involves a conflicting pull of different loyalties. Family blood ties are strong, and no one wants to upset family members. But a married couple's primary human loyalty should be to each other and to the marriage itself. Other family ties, and all that goes with that, should become secondary.

What is the best approach to stop parental interference? If a husband's mother-in-law is causing the problem, then his wife should be the one to tell her mother to back off. If a wife's mother-in-law is becoming a wedge in the marriage, then her husband should be the one to tell his mother to stop it. You need to be kind and gentle but pointed and firm. Never allow these interferences by one of your parents to disrupt your marriage.

This also applies to a situation involving any other relative. If one of your relatives is a thorn in the flesh of your wounded marriage, then pull that thorn out. Otherwise the wounded marriage may never be healed. You have the power and the right to do that. Whatever you do, however, do it together in unity and do it in love (even if it's *tough love*).

# 14

## The Job

All marriages are impacted to one degree or another by the husband's job outside the home, the wife's job, or both. No longer is the husband's job always the focus of a marriage.

### Dual-Earner Marriages

Women now make up a major portion of the labor force in the United States. Today approximately 56 percent of women are working outside of the home, with about half of those women being mothers with children at home. Women also own almost three of every ten small businesses, indicating that they are taking a more aggressive role in the labor force. It is becoming quite common today to observe many women in business and professional leadership roles.[16]

However, women going to work in such numbers and in increasingly high-level positions often leads to considerable worry, tension, and exhaustion. A *New York*

*Times* poll of working women recently revealed that 83 percent felt pulled between the pressures of their jobs and the desire to be a better mother in rearing their children at home. These women identified the number-one problem they faced as the tension between their job and their family.[17]

So a wounded marriage can result when a wife spends so much of her time and energy in gainful employment away from home that she comes home at the end of the day physically, mentally, and emotionally exhausted. Since her husband may also come home exhausted, both are tired and unable to focus on each other. There is very little energy or will left to focus on maintaining and enriching the marital relationship. Then if the couple's spending habits exceed the husband's income and he insists that she go to work to make ends meet, she may come to resent him for putting them both in this predicament.

The truth of the matter is, however, that given the typically high materialistic goals of most American couples in the latter part of the twentieth century, few husbands can earn enough by themselves to pay the bills. So often the wife is just as much to blame as he is that they are in such financial straits that a second income is perceived as an absolute necessity.

Most of the families I have worked with as a pastor appeared to me as too busy, too overly committed to their jobs, too tired at the end of the day, and too emotionally worn out to be able to have a relaxed and enjoyable relationship in the evenings and on weekends at home. Under those stressed-out conditions, no wonder their marriage takes a beating. Work-induced neglect of the marriage is the inevitable result. Stressed-out couples can easily turn on and emotionally injure each other.

# The Job 91

## The Workaholic

A very common problem I see in wounded marriages is when the husband is a workaholic.[18] In effect, he is so committed to his job, to making a success of his career, and to making more money that his relationship with his wife suffers. From the wife's perspective, it is almost as though her husband is married to his job, or as one frustrated wife told me, "It's like I'm competing with another woman—except in this case her name is *Job*."

I've counseled many wives whose husbands are scientists and engineers with various Department of Energy laboratories. These men sometimes work between twelve and sixteen hours a day for several months on a high-pressure project with a next-to-impossible deadline. Such wives can quickly become extremely frustrated that they see so little of their husband at home. Practically speaking, the husband's job comes first, and his wife feels that she comes second or third in his list of priorities. Such men often go to bed so tired that they don't even have the energy or forethought to kiss their wife good night.

## Importance of Work versus Relationships

Generally speaking, men are more identified with their work than women are. There are notable exceptions in a growing number of women who are successful attorneys, judges, CEOs, corporation board members, military personnel, educators, medical doctors and other medical specialists, bankers, stockbrokers, entrepreneurial businesswomen, ministers, and airline pilots. However, in American culture the self-image of a man is more related to his work position, while a woman's self-image is more often based on relationships. This is one reason it can be very traumatic for a husband to discover that his wife holds a more prestigious job and makes more money than he does.

*J. C. was a traveling salesman whose income would be considered average. His wife, Cynthia, was a veteran nurse in a local hospital who had moved up through the ranks. One day she came home and announced that she was promoted to Chief of Nursing for the hospital with a salary several thousand dollars a year more than J. C. earned in his job. He was devastated. Instead of rejoicing with her over her accomplishment and appreciating the additional income, J. C. considered himself a failure. As a result, their marriage suffered. He resented her success. He became sexually impotent, and it took many hours of counseling to work through his feelings and to accept her advancement.*

## Financial Strain

Some marriages are wounded either because the husband seldom seems to hold onto a job for any length of time or because the jobs he does get simply do not pay enough to provide for the family. If the wife is the mother of preschoolers and wants to stay home with them, she may resent the fact that out of dire necessity she must go to work to provide for the basics. Subconsciously she may blame her husband for the financial hardships they constantly face.

Such women may demean their husband with comments such as:

"If you had only gone to college . . ."

"If you only had the motivation to get those specialized skills needed to get the better jobs . . ."

"If you weren't so lazy . . ."

"If you really cared about us . . ."

"I wouldn't have to work if you would get off your duff and get a decent job."

Such words do not make for a good relationship.

## Constant Moves

Other marriages suffer when the husband's work calls for occasional if not regular transfers to distant cities. Moving often can be very stressful for a relationship. Especially for a family with children, putting roots down and establishing some long-term relationships are important stabilizers for a home. Jobs related to the military services, national corporations, or church ministry often call for moving in order to move up the ladder.

Women tend to be more attached to their home than men are. After getting the house in order, decorating it just right, putting in a yard and garden, and helping the children establish some sense of "my territory," it is very depressing for a wife to hear her husband announce that he is being transferred to another city. When the job situation doesn't give you a choice—either move with the company or quit—a man can feel trapped between the wishes of his wife and children and the requirements of his job.

Sometimes the problem is simply that the husband has wanderlust. Psychologically, he can't seem to settle down anywhere for long. He is restless and has difficulty committing himself for the long haul in whatever line of work he is in. He lacks "stick-ability." Or, he may be a dreamer, always searching for greener pastures. If this instability is related to irresponsibility and insecurity, a wife may finally conclude that she married the wrong man.

## Balanced Perspective

Couples need to thoroughly discuss the job—both his and hers. Before marriage, the vocational plans of both should be explained and accepted. A new job should not be accepted until there is a clear understanding of what is expected and required of you. Take charge of your life and refuse to surrender to being the victim of vocational circumstances. The job should be seen as a means, never as an end in itself. Your marriage and family are more important than any job, including the ministry. What kind of wisdom is it that succeeds at work but fails at home?

If one or both of you are going into a vocation that calls for high geographical mobility, then decide in advance whether you are willing to do this, and if so, then prepare psychologically and spiritually to make the necessary adjustments.

Always keep your job in a servant role, never in a master role. The concept of a divine *calling* has helped many people to keep their job situation in a properly balanced perspective. This does not apply merely to the religious vocational ministry. John Calvin and other Protestant Reformers have helped us tremendously to understand that the biblical teaching of vocation (calling) can apply to any line of work that contributes constructively to society and is morally above reproach. Calvin taught that work should be a means of glorifying God. But, I would add, it should also be a means of strengthening your marriage, not destroying it.

If your job is wounding your marriage, then either change your perspective and your priorities or change jobs.

# 15

# The Finances

It is sometimes said that the three most critical problem areas for marriage are money, sex, and friends. Although I believe that personality differences and different levels of maturity are more influential in rocking the boat of a marriage, wounded marriages certainly have more than their share of major injuries suffered on the battlefield of finances. Earning and spending money seem to be potential catalysts for disrupting what might otherwise be a good marriage.

## Conflicting Family Values

Your family background has a lot to do with developing your attitude toward finances.

*Beth and Roger seemed to get off to a good start in their early days of marriage. But before long their different family backgrounds began to show up in their feelings over handling money. Beth's family*

95

*had always been on the very edge of poverty. Her father never finished high school, and her mother never moved past the eighth grade. Consequently, their earning power was severely diminished due to a lack in saleable skills in the job market. Roger's family was clearly in the middle-class business sector of the community.*

*Beth's family seemed never to have any money left over each month to save for the future. Their attitude was that money was to be spent until it was gone. They lived from paycheck to paycheck. They never learned the value of being frugal. Roger's family, although not considered wealthy by any means, held to standard middle-class values of hard work, frugality, investment, and saving for the future. They emphasized saving more than spending.*

*Beth and Roger learned these different sets of values from their respective families. Shopping in the grocery store, Beth was more of a compulsive buyer, which resulted in more spending than necessary. Roger was the one who cut out discount grocery coupons in the newspaper and magazines and who insisted on making a list of what was actually needed from the store.*

*Also, it never occurred to Beth that making long-distance telephone calls in the daytime hours during weekdays resulted in paying the highest calling rates. Roger insisted that calling in the evenings and on weekends would save considerably on the phone bill. Since Beth's mother tended to call during high-rate hours, Beth felt that calling impulsively was more important than saving money. After all, "money is to be spent, not saved." For Beth and her family, spending what little money they had on each other was an important way to say "I love you."*

*At one point in their marriage, Roger felt that Beth should become familiar with their finances by keeping the books and paying the bills. He had read that every husband should prepare his wife for becoming a widow someday. He realized that if something happened to him and Beth was forced to take charge of the finances, she would be totally unprepared to manage. So he introduced Beth to the family book-keeping, monthly obligations, income, and checkbook procedures. However, when Beth took over, her old family economic values went into effect again. She tended to spend more than they earned each month. Borrowing, charging, and paying high interest became the pattern of family finances after a while.*

*All of these various value differences soon became a serious bone of contention for Roger and Beth. Roger became frustrated, irritated, and angry over Beth's freewheeling spending and disinterest in frugality. There were things Roger wanted to do and places he wanted to go, but there never was any money left over for such extras. As Roger commented, "Beth has thrown it away." He aggravated the situation by often saying to her, "No wonder your parents were always broke and dependent on someone else to bail them out of debt!"*

Beth and Roger represent the extremes of frugality and extravagance, conservatism and wastefulness operating in the same marriage. Somehow they needed to learn how to meet in the middle: Beth needed to learn how to tighten up, while Roger needed to learn how to loosen up. Unless they could learn to change, their strained relationship would continue to deteriorate over the years.

## Uninformed Wives

Another potential area of conflict can be the practice of a husband keeping his wife uninformed about family finances. Most husbands will die before their wife does, and an increasing number of women realize this to the point that a gnawing insecurity can begin to affect the relationship. Even working wives with fairly good incomes know that if they lost their husband's income, it would be very difficult to make ends meet or at least to maintain their accustomed standard of living.

Middle-aged and older married women may ask themselves, "What will I do if my husband becomes unexpectedly disabled or dies before he retires?" Deep-seated worry can set in that will adversely affect the marriage. Some married women do not even know where their husband's insurance policies are located, much less what the total amount of the payoff would be. Some wives may ask their husband about such matters, but too often the response is, "Oh, I've taken care of everything, so don't worry about it. Just trust me." Some couples do not even have joint wills prepared, and it is normal for a woman to be deeply concerned about this.

Most women have a basic need for security, and unanswered questions and lack of information can be very unsettling when they contemplate the worst-case scenario of the loss of a major source of income. Most women, therefore, look to their husband to make certain that the wife and young children will be cared for in the future, come what may. A cavalier attitude here on the part of the husband may cause the wife to wonder, "Does he really love me (us)?" Financial insecurity can make marital intimacy very difficult for a woman. Consequently, arguments, threats, pressure, and questioning of love and protection can easily ensue over family finances, resulting in serious emotional injuries to the relationship.

## A Blessing, Not a Curse

How can finances in a marriage become a blessing rather than a curse? Consider the following suggestions if you would like to keep finances from wounding your marriage.

1. *Identify and seriously examine your cultural values related to money, wealth, and possessions.* If you are a Christian, it will be helpful for you to compare these values (brought into your marriage from your past) with the biblical principles of stewardship. God teaches us in the Bible that what money we earn and save is not his, hers, or ours,

# The Finances

but it is God's! That is, all belongs to God, and he has simply entrusted a portion to us to manage as his stewards. We are managers, not owners. Moreover, we are accountable to God for how we use the money he enables us to earn. Consequently, a spirit of "managerial sensitivity" takes over.

2. *Commit yourselves early in the marriage to plan wisely never to spend more than you earn.* There will be some major purchases (such as a house, a car, or some land) that will require a loan to be paid off over a period of time, so you will want to budget these payments within your estimated income.

Related to this, it is important, especially for young and inexperienced couples, to avoid the *credit card trap*. Many couples have crashed financially because they could not resist the overuse of "plastic money." Although it is very tempting to use these readily available cards, it is important to remember that a charge on a credit card is borrowing money at the highest possible interest rate.

Wise financial counselors suggest that couples use credit cards only for a few routine expenses where writing a check is not possible or not the best option: for example, auto gasoline charges, airline tickets with automatic life insurance coverage, car rentals, and others. Credit cards should never be used for such items as groceries and clothes. Pay as you go.

3. *The Bible teaches us to tithe our income to the Lord.* As Christians we should set aside 10 percent each month for the Lord's work. Jesus taught, "Where your treasure is, there your heart will be also" (Matt. 6:21). I have discovered that there is a powerful psychological dynamic at work in the practice of tithing: We take seriously the beneficial process of careful management that impacts the handling of the remaining 90 percent as well. Tithing starts us and keeps us on the road to better management of all our God-provided resources.

4. *Seek good financial advice early in your marriage.* However, even if you've been married several years, it's never too late to get some specific help regarding finances. Most banks and financial institutions provide free financial counseling for their regular customers. If you're already over your heads in debt, ask your bank for help and then ask your creditors for advice and a plan for getting out of debt.

In addition, there are some very helpful books on the market dealing with financial responsibility from a Christian point of view. Authors such as Ron Blue and Larry Burkett have written extremely helpful materials for married couples. These can go a long way in helping to heal wounded marriages with financial injuries.[19] Several financial plan books for families are also available.[20] Finally, ask your church to sponsor a family financial management seminar led by a competent professional at least once each year.

# 16

# The Church

Is it possible? The church a contributing factor in a wounded marriage? Unfortunately, yes! A Christian couple can be so overly committed and involved in their church that their marriage can suffer under the stress of overcommitment. Or, in a marriage where one spouse is a Christian and the other is not, the church can at times be allowed to become a wedge in the relationship.

## Dominance/Submission

In addition, there are some churches where the preaching and teaching ministry conveys the idea that the husband should be the boss (head) of the wife, while the wife is to be the obedient and passive, subservient partner. This view is usually based upon a gross misinterpretation of Ephesians 5:22–24, which nearly always ignores the larger context of Ephesians 5:15–33, which clearly teaches *mutual submis-*

*sion,* whereby both husband and wife should serve each other in equality by meeting each other's needs in mutual respect and complementariness. Paul teaches this in the context of instructing Christians on how to be filled with the Holy Spirit.

A growing number of intelligent, Christian women are becoming deeply resentful of the dominant/submissive marital motif that is taught in many ultraconservative churches. This motif actually reflects more of a pagan view of marriage than a Christian one. In Matthew 20:25–28 Jesus told his followers that they were to relate to others as servants, not lording it over their subservients as the pagan rulers did. An implication follows that when a Christian husband lords it over his wife, he is acting more like a pagan than a Christian.

The "new Christian women" are seeing themselves as the equals of men as taught in Genesis 1:26–27, where it is obvious that both men and women are equally created in the image of God. One is not superior to the other; rather, each complements the other as is also brought out in Genesis 2:18–25. Recent conservative biblical scholarship has brought out the teachings of complementariness and equality. Christian women who are well read in recent biblical studies now know this and deeply resent being put down by preachers who espouse the antiquated dominance/submission motif.[21]

Recent research has shown that wife abuse sometimes follows close on the heels of the espoused philosophy of the submission of women to their domineering husbands. That is, some husbands use the dominance/submission motif to justify abusing their wife.[22] Churches need to be very careful about what they teach regarding husband and wife relationships.

# The Church

## Putting the Church First

Vocational Christian workers in the church (pastors and other full-time church staff members) can easily fall into the trap of allowing their overcommitment to the church to become a major problem in their marriage. Ministers, whatever their formal position, can carelessly put the church above their marriage and family, assuming such priorities have a divine blessing. After all, some think, "God called me to this work, and my calling comes first."

We sometimes hear a very foolish and unbiblical prioritizing of life's duties: "God first, the church second, and my marriage or family third." Such a view of life inadvertently places an unChristian guilt trip on couples who honestly want to serve the Lord even when it strains their marriage. It is my conviction that we properly put God first when we put our vocation and marriage into proper perspective, which calls for a balanced emphasis of being both a responsible minister and a responsible husband or wife, father or mother. This balancing of life's responsibilities would include laypersons as well because, after all, the Bible views all Christians as ministers in the broad sense (see Eph. 4:11–13).

## Non-Christian Spouse

One of the most common situations of a marriage being wounded by the church is the case of a Christian being married to a non-Christian.

*Cecilia, a very devout Christian and active member of her church, came to me for counseling quite distressed that her husband, Martin, would have nothing to do with her church. She had only been a Christian for about a year, and she and Martin had been married for over five years. Cecilia was so excited over her newfound faith that she honestly believed that Martin would see the difference in her and become a Christian himself. However, Martin's response was belligerent resistance.*

*Every Sunday morning Cecilia would invite and encourage Martin to go to church with her. His negative response would motivate Cecilia to attempt to witness to him about his need to become a follower of Christ. After several attempts at this, Martin began to become aggravated with his wife's efforts to convert him. He considered her new religious zeal as going overboard and thought she was becoming a religious fanatic.*

*Martin often responded that he believed in God but that the church was not for him. He claimed that as a boy he and his family had had a bad experience with a church in their hometown that he did not want to talk about. He had come to conclude that all churches were like that one. "All they want is your money," he would say.*

*This difference of opinion over religion and the church brought considerable stress into the marriage of Cecilia and Martin. Martin's perception was that religion was turning his wife into a bossy and nagging woman. Cecilia viewed Martin as insensitive and unappreciative of her new relationship with God and the church. Such religious conflict made marital intimacy difficult. The relationship was hurting.*

*Cecilia was greatly helped when she was asked to make a study of 1 Peter 3:1–6, where the apostle advises a Christian wife to follow the example of Jesus (explained and applied in 1 Peter 2) and submit to her husband with respectful reverence, using behavior rather than words to win a non-Christian spouse. That is, the purity and reverence of the wife's actions are a more powerful witness than argumentative words. Such submission does not imply any inferiority in the wife, but a wiser approach to witnessing. It is impossible for a non-Christian spouse to argue with or resent a loving spirit reflected in deeds of kindness and respect. In the end, this is what usually wins a spouse over.*

# The Church

*In Cecilia's case, this took longer than she wanted it to. But coupled with prayer and faith, this better approach was used by God to win Martin to Christ and the church.*

Are you in a hurry? Do you want instant results? Ask God for patience, and then prayerfully follow Jesus' example as you seek to win your spouse to Christ and heal your marriage.

## Strengthen Your Marriage

If you are too busy at the church, you will be wise to back off and reexamine the nature and extent of your commitment. Couples can be devout Christians without being at the church every time the doors are open. It helps to see the church like a cafeteria: Take want you want and need and leave the rest to others. Decide what you have to give—not just your money, but your talents and giftedness as well—and make the most of that. You can't do everything! Don't even try. The church should be seen as a means and never as an end in itself.

Know your gifts, abilities, and interests. Decide what God has called you to do. Learn to say "no" when you need to and "yes" when the opportunities fit your spiritual gifts. The church is a means to assist your spiritual growth as an individual and as a couple. That applies to whether you are the pastor and wife or a lay couple.

If your church's teachings regarding marriage are of the dominance/submission motif and this is putting stress on your relationship, then find a church that teaches mutual servanthood for Christian couples. Christian couples who engage in a Christlike relationship that goes beyond equality and companionship to mutual and cooperative ministry as a couple tend to be much more satisfied with that kind of relationship. As Christians, you both have been created in the image of God and have been called into a cooperative expression of practical ministry that begins at home and yet is channeled in and through a local church.

There is absolutely no need for a church to be an instrument for wounding your marriage. If your church is a wounding one and won't change, then change churches. The church can and should be the best institutional friend your marriage has.

If the problem is with you, then make the necessary changes in your attitudes and beliefs about Christian faith, Christian marriage, and your behavior. This will probably call for a reworking of your priorities regarding church involvement. After all, when you strengthen your marriage, you strengthen your church. I wish all churches would learn this truth.

# 17

# The Bible

The Bible is the Word of God and the recorded revelation from God as to how to get to know God through Jesus Christ and how to live the Christian life. But the Bible can also be misused as an instrument for wounding a marriage. This was pointed out briefly in the last chapter regarding some churches that teach the dominance/submission motif as the ideal Christian marriage. The Bible is God's truth, but it needs to be properly interpreted. It is relatively easy to misquote the Bible and make it say what it doesn't really teach.

*Joe and Mary Lou were members of a Bible study class in an ultraconservative church in the Midwest. Their teacher, Scott, was a sincere Christian who honestly believed that the best way to interpret all texts in the Bible was the* literal *approach. Believing that* literal *and* true *were synonymous terms in biblical interpretation, and not understanding the wide variety of literary forms in the Bible, Scott took certain texts dealing with marriage and family and taught his literalist view as the only way to understand them.*

*For example, Scott interpreted Ephesians 5:22–23, "Wives, submit to your husbands as to the Lord. For the husband is the head of the wife. . . ." without reference either to the total context (Eph. 5:15–6:9) or to the immediate context (Eph. 5:21–33). This approach ignores that Paul is giving instructions on how to be filled with the Holy Spirit (see Eph. 5:18), which is done by being submissive "to one another out of reverence for Christ" (Eph. 5:21). Paul then applies this concept of mutual submission or servanthood to wives and husbands* equally *but in different terms.*

*Scott's approach also ignored the very important qualifiers in the passage: "as Christ," which sets forth the criteria—the how-to of being mutually submissive. Scott's dominance/submission approach was really no different than the standard pagan view as revealed in the Greco-Roman and Jewish cultures of that day. Jesus gives us insight into those views in Matthew 20:25, where he reminds us that non-Christians "lord it over" others and "exercise authority over them." Then in the next verse he decrees that such an approach must not be exercised by his followers. Rather, following his example, Christians must be servants to one another.*

*Unfortunately, Joe and Mary Lou weren't taught this more balanced view of Paul's teaching. Consequently, Joe felt that the Christian way to behave as the "head" of his wife was to make all the decisions and, if necessary, command her to do what was right as he saw it. Mary Lou was to be his submissive wife and obey whatever Joe said to do. She was never to question Joe's word. To do so would mean she was disobeying God's Word. It seemed that she was to look upon Joe as if he were God, because God had authorized Joe to speak for him.*

*Later, Joe learned that* head *in Scripture is the English translation of a Greek word that can mean*

1. *the literal, anatomical head of a body*
2. *the top of anything*
3. *the first in a series*
4. *a leader*
5. *the source of something*[23]

# The Bible
## 109

*We use the word today similarly as in*

1. *the physical head*
2. *the head of the line*
3. *a leader of a group*
4. *the source of a river (e.g., the headwaters)*

*Eventually Joe came to recognize that he was the source of Mary Lou's "wifeness" and therefore was responsible for her, and that his role as leader should be qualified by Christ's example of servanthood. However, this new insight did not come easily.[24]*

*In her heart, Mary Lou knew that Joe was not infallible and that some of his decisions were clearly unwise and unfair. She also realized that in some matters of daily living, she was far wiser and more experienced than Joe, especially when it came to matters related to the children. Teacher Scott's literal approach to the Bible had set up Mary Lou for a great deal of internal and unspoken resentment coupled with much guilt if she ever differed with Joe. According to Joe and Scott, Mary Lou was never to hold an opinion that differed from her husband's.*

*In time, this set the stage for considerable stress that eventually exploded in disagreements and long-standing arguments. One especially delicate matter that illustrates this was related to their sexual life. Joe believed that if he wanted to have sex with Mary Lou, she should be willing, even eager, to cooperate whether she felt like it or not. This demand for sex on Joe's part eventually destroyed all semblances of intimacy in their relationship. One night Mary Lou's resentment exploded with the verbal blast that she felt like Joe's "captive whore"—damaging language, to say the least.*

*Joe knew very little about the importance of preparing for intimacy in the following ways:*

- *your attitude and conversation during the day*
- *your tone of voice*

110  Re-Igniting Love and Passion

- *the respectful, nonverbal communication of caring, affectionate touching or hugging that has no sexual overtones*
- *the little considerations of the day that say "I love you" in numerous ways (i.e., helping to set the table for supper, clearing the table and cleaning up in the kitchen, helping with some of the housework, spending time with the children to give their mother some relief, and so on)*

*Consequently, Joe couldn't understand why Mary Lou felt put-upon all day long and resentful when they went to bed.*

*This dominance/submission pattern was reinforced often by Scott's teaching regarding other texts from the Bible, especially 1 Peter 3:1–6. Overlooking the fact that this passage was aimed at a particular problem of a Christian wife relating to a non-Christian husband, Scott put special emphasis on wives being submissive (v. 1), being a quiet example of purity and reverence (vv. 1–2, 4), hoping in God (v. 5) whenever, as Scott said, "things get tough," and following Sarah's example of obeying her husband (Abraham) and even calling him "her master" (v. 6). This example, he said, will guide a wife to do "what is right" and not be afraid (v. 6). Scott taught that this must be the norm for all wives in whatever situation they find themselves.*

*Joe understood all of this to mean he was the boss in the family—interpreting the Bible through a modern American culture motif ("boss") rather than allowing the Bible to speak for itself. The problem was that after Mary Lou had spent a few years tolerating Joe's bossiness, most intimacy and respect for him had flown out the marital window.*

*Fortunately, Mary Lou began to study the Bible for herself and discovered many interesting truths that Scott never brought out in their class. For example, she learned that both man and woman are created equally in the image of God (Gen. 1:27). One is not superior to the other: "This is now bone of my bones and flesh of my flesh" (Gen. 2:23)—you can't get any more equal than that! Actually, the woman was made to complement the man; this*

# The Bible

*complementariness is based upon the fact of equality ("a helper suitable for him," Gen. 2:18). Mary Lou also learned that the term* helper *is not a term of inferiority but is sometimes used to describe God himself (see Ps. 54:4).*

*Moreover, Mary Lou learned that one of Scott's favorite texts, Genesis 3:16 ("Your desire will be for your husband, and he will rule over you"), was given* after *Adam and Eve fell into sin and was a result of their sin. This text was descriptive and not prescriptive. Consequently, she realized that for a Christian husband to attempt to rule over his wife was to perpetuate the effects of the Fall and to fail to realize that now, "in Christ," Christian couples live in a "new creation" where "the old has gone, the new has come!" (2 Cor. 5:17).*

*It was not easy to confront Scott with the fact that he was misinterpreting the Bible to his class and misleading Joe to misapply these texts related to marriage. One very helpful book that opened Mary Lou's eyes to what the Bible actually teaches was* How to Read the Bible for All Its Worth, *by Gordon D. Fee and Douglas Stuart.*[25] *When she asked Joe to read it, he felt threatened, because he knew that if he began to read the Bible in a new light, he might have to change his views and his behavior.*

*However, after spending a couple of weeks reading Fee and Stuart, it began to dawn on Joe that the Bible is a book of liberation not bondage, that sound principles of interpretation are necessary to properly understand Scripture, and that when Jesus is truly Lord of your life and your marriage, then* dominance *and* submission *are irrelevant terms. Mutual servanthood began to make sense in light of the fact that every Christian marriage has a divine mission beyond equality and companionship.*

*Getting Scott to read Fee and Stuart was even more difficult for Mary Lou and Joe. Scott felt extremely threatened in view of the fact that he was their teacher. If he had been grossly misinterpreting the Bible, he would have to admit it before the entire class and would lose face. Yet Scott was big enough to admit that truth should prevail regardless of what it did to his ego. After all, a primary purpose of Bible study is to subject ourselves to its power to change our lives and stimulate us to grow. Scott's change of convictions was both painful and liberating.*

*One real test of whether you are interpreting the Bible properly is the final outcome in whether it strengthens or weakens your marriage. When Scott and the other members of their Bible class saw the beneficial consequences to Joe and Mary Lou's marriage when they applied the principle of mutual servanthood, especially in the lessening of marital stress and the increasing of mutual respect and appreciation for each other, they began to realize that the liberation principle is much more Christian than the domination principle. Christ has liberated Christian couples to be free, mutual, and complementary servants to one another.*

# 18

# The Stress

A certain amount of stress is normal and acceptable in our lives. Moderate amounts of stress motivate us to fulfill most of the daily obligations involved in normal living, including getting up and going to work on time.

However, a wounded marriage experiences a considerable amount of stress, and too much stress can be very damaging both to the marital relationship and to your physical health. If you are in a wounded marriage, you are doubtless experiencing a burdensome degree of stress, evidenced by the wear and tear you feel on your life.

What do we mean by *stress?* Hans Selye, noted biologist with the Institute of Experimental Medicine and Surgery at the University of Montreal, has defined stress as "the nonspecific response of the body to any demand made upon it." He goes on to say that stress is essentially the wear and tear of living.[26]

113

There are four things we can say about stress:

1. It is the exhausting effects of life's heaviest demands.
2. It is a state manifested by a specific syndrome of biological events and can be both pleasant and unpleasant.
3. It is the mobilization of the body's defenses that allow human beings to adapt to hostile or threatening events.
4. It can be dangerous when it is unduly prolonged, comes too often, or concentrates on one particular organ of the body.

On the other hand, we can say that stress is *not:*

1. merely nervous tension,
2. the discharge of hormones from the adrenal glands,
3. the influence of some negative occurrence, or
4. an entirely bad event or experience.

Researchers have identified three stages of stress following a threatening experience:

1. The alarm stage—the body prepares itself for fight or flight survival.
2. The resistance stage—the body returns to normality.
3. The exhaustion stage—prolonged stress begins to affect some organs of the body adversely (e.g., hypertension, heart attack, ulcers, skin rashes).

Jeanne Anselmo, B.S.N., R.N., a stress management and biofeedback consultant, has prepared a helpful chart entitled "Dealing with Stress—Healthful Tips." She defines *stress* as "tension or pressures that are a natural part of living our lives. Changes and events in our lives . . . are a major source of stress. Pressures and tension from both good and bad changes can trigger our Stress Alarm System making us feel that we want to either fight the stress or run away from it."

# The Stress

Anselmo goes on to say that you can know if you are having a stress reaction by learning to read your mind and body language: cold hands, rapid breathing, rapid heartbeat, anxiety, forgetfulness, shakiness, headaches, muscle tension, knotted stomach. These symptoms let you know you need to change the stress, leave the stress, or go with it. You also need to be alert for stress symptoms if you undergo several changes in a short period of time. These changes do not have to be major (e.g., death of a loved one); minor changes, even happy ones, can lead to illness if they occur often within a short span of time.[27]

Other signs of stress can be: difficulty in sleeping, changes in eating habits, increased use of drugs (even prescription drugs), excessive use of alcohol and/or cigarettes, chronic irritability, short-fused anger, increased anxiety, and frequent illness or physical complaints.

Public school teacher and author Dolores Curran has identified ten top family stresses. These are the areas where we experience the most stress in a marital or family situation:

1. economics, finances, budgeting
2. children's behavior, discipline, sibling fighting
3. insufficient couple time
4. lack of shared responsibility in the family
5. communicating with children
6. insufficient "me" time
7. guilt for not accomplishing more
8. spousal relationship (communication, friendship, sex)
9. insufficient family playtime
10. overscheduled family calendar[28]

Such a list can help you better come to grips with stress in your marriage or at least identify the possible causes and focus your relief efforts there.

Psychiatrist Keith Sehnert has identified certain social or cultural causes of marital and family stress:

1. Geographical mobility: Americans move a lot, and this involves losses of familiar faces, friends, places, pleasure, ways of doing things, and organizational supports (e.g., a familiar church).
2. Changing family roles: The meaning of *husband, wife, father, mother, maleness, femaleness* are in flux to a large degree. Role change is "the single most outstanding phenomenon of this century," says Sehnert.
3. The changing nature of work: large companies, impersonal relations, frequent job changes, weak loyalties.
4. Erosion of traditions: play, education, courtship, jobs, role of the church, religious traditions of family.
5. Modern conveniences: automobile (traffic stress), kitchen appliances (less exercise, more body weight, resulting in poor health), television (sedentary lifestyle, less interaction).

Sehnert concludes that our modern society has lost many of the supports, traditions, and convictions that have helped America to become great and allowed its people to survive with peace of mind, and these continue to diminish in recent years.[29]

*The stress felt in a typical wounded marriage could be illustrated by the marriage of Boyd and Frances. Their stressors included the following:*

- *Although both worked long hours away from home to make ends meet, their expenses were always greater than their income.*

# The Stress 117

- *Boyd felt that sex cures everything, which resulted in an unhealthy overemphasis on sex.*
- *One of their children had A.D.D. (attention deficit disorder) and was constantly interrupting any family tranquility.*
- *Boyd and Frances had strong religious differences.*
- *Boyd was always threatening to leave Frances if she didn't meet his expectations.*
- *They showed a general unwillingness to talk over their problems.*

*Marriage for Boyd and Frances was no longer any fun. They were completely stressed out, and the wounds were deep. They felt helpless.*

If your marriage is wounded by stress, there are a number of things you can do to help yourself: First, get a thorough physical examination to determine whether any medical condition is causing or adding to your stress. Then seek professional counseling from a qualified psychological therapist. You can also benefit from stress management and relaxation programs provided at work, community mental health centers, and adult education programs.

Anselmo's suggestions for handling stress include:[30]

1. Don't fool yourself—drugs, tobacco, and alcohol are no cure for stress. Medications, such as tranquilizers and sleeping pills, should only be used under a doctor's prescription. Drugs do not deal with the source of stress, and frequent or long-term use can lead to drug dependence.
2. The stress inside you—thoughts and feelings—can build up tension. Learning how to be assertive, expressing your feelings (sadness, joy, hurt, anger, excitement), and learning from past experiences can

help relieve stress inside you. What worked for you? What do you need to change or learn more about? Who can help you learn?

3. You spend the largest part of your day on the job. If you find yourself starting to rush or panic—STOP, take a deep breath, and give yourself time to think things through and quiet down. Instead of your usual coffee or smoke break, take a relaxation break and stretch or walk around. Prevent burnout by taking the first half-hour at home to unwind from work before starting your *home* work with spouse and children.

4. Develop a realistic, positive attitude. Recognizing when you are being unfair or unrealistic with yourself is a good start. Be alert to traps such as, "I have to . . . ," "I must . . . ," "I can't . . . ," "If only . . ." Give yourself *self-applause*, a pat on the back for a job well done, and look for the positive in any failure—ask yourself what you have learned from this experience.

5. Relax. Relaxation is a skill in itself. Listening to soft music, exercise, daydreaming, taking time to "smell the roses," and meditation can help the mind and body quiet down so you feel renewed. Imagery (picturing a quiet scene with all your senses—what it looks like, smells like, tastes like, feels like, sounds like) helps your mind to reprogram itself to being able to relax at will. (Incidentally, this is *not* New Age theology. Long ago, the Bible spoke of dreams and visions—Joel 2:28; Acts 2:17.)

6. Get proper rest and sleep. This gives your mind (and body) time to quiet down and regenerate. Getting seven to eight hours of sleep at least three times a week helps. If stress is affecting your sleep try (1) drinking some warm milk, (2) writing down all the things cluttering your mind, and (3) stretching and

# The Stress

119

taking a warm bath with relaxing music before going to bed.

Of course, it is best to prevent stress before it happens. To do this, Anselmo suggests the following:[31]

1. Eat right. Foods high in protein, vitamin C, B vitamins, and vitamin A protect us from the effects of stress. These are found in whole grain products, fruits and vegetables (especially citrus fruits and dark green vegetables), meat, and dairy products. Avoid caffeine (in colas, chocolate, tea, and coffee), refined sugars, starches, and junk food since they create false energy and stress the body even more.
2. Manage time better. Take five minutes at the beginning of each day and make a things-to-do list. Convert this list into a priority list of primary tasks, secondary tasks, and miscellaneous tasks. Do primary tasks first and continue until the list is finished. Don't overschedule—leave time for unexpected events. Reward yourself for a job well done.
3. Exercise your tension away. You feel healthier and less stressed when you develop an exercise plan that meets your lifestyle, needs, and ability. Stretching exercises are good for developing flexibility and relaxation. Aerobic exercise, swimming, jogging, tennis, and biking are good for cardiovascular fitness. Exercise for twenty minutes at least three times a week, but check with your doctor before starting any exercise program.

Another important aspect in healing a wounded, overstressed marriage is to deal with your spiritual need. Engage in a daily quiet time, reading the Bible and praying each morning or evening. Faithfully attend Sunday morning worship at your church as a couple. Seek out or organize a small support group of Christian friends in your church that will meet once a week for a few months at a time. And most importantly, begin practicing the presence of God in your daily life.

*When Boyd and Frances began this program of stress relief, they had a long way to go. In counseling, however, they agreed that their marriage was more important than anything that would disrupt it, so they committed themselves to the task of coping with their stress factors. These specific steps made sense to them, and over time, they found that they worked.*

# 19

# The Doctor

Most every wounded marriage eventually involves a doctor either directly or indirectly. This may be a family practice (primary care) physician or a specialist, such as a psychiatrist, gynecologist, or a counselor in clinical psychology. Participants in a wounded marriage will eventually hurt enough to go to a professional for help.

Since the emotional and relational wounds in an injured marriage often erupt into physical symptoms of one sort or another, a wounded spouse will often turn to his or her family physician for treatment and advice. Most family physicians are well aware of the marital problems of many of their patients, which evidence themselves through secondary symptoms or primary symptoms.

The *secondary* symptoms include a variety of physical problems such as skin rashes, high blood pressure, digestive problems, sleeplessness, sexual impotence (male), sexual frigidity (female), migraine headaches, heart palpitations or other cardiac irregularities, chronic depression, prescription drug abuse, or any one of a variety of psychosomatic illnesses. Although the physician may be able to treat the symptoms effectively, if the root cause is not identified and dealt with, the symptoms may eventually return.

The *primary* symptoms of a wounded marriage sometimes seen in the doctor's office include direct physical and/or emotional abuse on the part of one or both of the spouses. Family violence in the United States today is considered by some family life experts as virtually epidemic. Physicians see the evidence of this almost daily. One expression of family violence is spouse abuse, which in most instances is wife abuse.

Some researchers estimate that wife abuse occurs at least once in two-thirds of all marriages, while others conclude that about a third of all wives are physically beaten at some time in the course of their marriage.[32] James and Phyllis Alsdurf, a clinical psychologist and his wife, note that physical abuse includes but is not limited to: hitting, shoving, pinching, pulling, bruising, biting, kicking, scratching, shooting, raping, and slapping. In addition, the Alsdurfs cite family issues researcher Kersti Yllo, who defines a violent act as one that is "carried out with the knowledge that the likely consequences of it will be physical injury or pain to another person."[33]

Jane O'Reilly, in one of a 1983 series of *Time* magazine articles dealing with domestic violence, noted: "Nearly 6 million wives will be abused by their husbands in any one year. Some 2,000 to 4,000 women are beaten to death annually. The nation's police spend one-third of their time responding to domestic violence calls. Battery is the single major cause of injury to women, more significant than accidents, rapes, or muggings."[34] If anything, these statistics have increased during the past decade.

Being professing Christians and active in a church does not automatically provide immunity from spouse abuse. As shown by the subtitle of their book, the research of the Alsdurfs focuses primarily on *The Tragedy of Wife Abuse in the*

# The Doctor 123

*Christian Home.* The gospel of Jesus Christ involves more than a name to bear and a religious activity in which to be engaged. One of the gospel's primary purposes is to penetrate to the very deepest level of your character so that your behavior is, sometimes gradually, sometimes suddenly, transformed radically in the direction of godly action. Since God is love, spouse abuse by professing Christians is a direct denial of Christian faith.

If you are the victim of spouse abuse to one degree or another, you have four alternatives in coping with this very serious problem:

1. You can stay in the marriage and remain unchanged. The result will be more battering and possibly a premature death. If nothing else, you will continue to be miserable.
2. You can stay in the marriage and change your response to your abusing spouse. You can determine not to put up with it, seek professional help, and report the abuse to the police. However, you can only change yourself. Your spouse may be unwilling to change, and a happy ending is not likely.
3. You can leave the marriage and remain unchanged yourself. This gets you out of the danger zone, but if you had been unknowingly contributing to the situation and you remarry and do not change, you may repeat your problem in a new marriage.
4. You can leave your spouse and change yourself. Here you remove yourself from the danger zone of abuse as well as concentrate on discovering the dynamics of your own personality that may need transformation. Then, whether you divorce your abusive spouse, remain single, remarry another person, or work diligently to save your marriage (by getting professional help for your spouse as well as yourself), you will be in

a better position to act out of wisdom as you set a new course for your life that will be free of abuse.[35]

Specifically, what can you do if you are in an abusive situation? Louisville hospital chaplain Wesley Monfalcone suggests the following steps:

1. Seek help from a support system (family members, doctors, social workers, carefully chosen friends, pastor, or a church-sponsored support group). If there seem to be none available to you, then create your own, possibly with your pastor's help. Discover others with similar problems and relate to them.
2. Get to safety and refuge such as a community-sponsored battered spouse shelter or an emotionally strong family member's home.
3. Seek counseling, preferably from a trained professional.

You may have to make several starts at leaving and beginning again . . . and again. Determine to make your own decisions and not just follow others' advice. Finally, take the first step. Seek God's help and get with it.[36]

Your family physician, medical specialist, and family counselor can be among the best friends of your wounded marriage. They are valuable resources of help, wisdom, and strength. They may refer you to other specialists (such as an attorney who is an expert in family law, a law enforcement specialist in domestic affairs, a social work specialist in marriage and family life, or a pastor who has clinical pastoral education training), but stay close to your family doctor, medical specialist, or clinical psychologist counselor for ongoing therapy and treatment for the long-term benefits.

It is clearer today than ever before that the physical body is intricately related to the relational and emotional experi-

# The Doctor 125

ences of life. A wounded marriage can damage your body. As a matter of fact, your heart will more than likely be one of the primary targets of a ruptured marital relationship. Clinical cardiologist Dr. Alexander Lowen, M.D., in his book, *Love, Sex, and Your Heart,* has shown in vivid detail that the connection between love and the heart is far more than symbolic—it is very real. Repressed emotions, especially unresolved sexual conflicts, and deep psychic hurts can actually rigidify the chest so that it becomes like an armored breastplate. This trapped emotional energy can literally constrict your heart and set you up for a heart attack.[37]

A wounded marriage, consequently, is more than merely an unhappy marriage. It is dangerous to your health! Therefore, it is strongly advisable to turn to your doctor as a beginning step toward healing not only the physical problems but also the root causes of the damaging relationship in which you find yourself.

The proverb, "For lack of guidance a nation falls, but many advisers make victory sure" (Prov. 11:14), also applies to a marriage in trouble.

# 20

## The Affair

Some wounded marriages have been significantly and negatively impacted by an extramarital affair. I wouldn't say that all of the woundedness is *caused* by an affair, because there are other long-standing factors that motivate one or both of the spouses to engage in an affair in the first place. But a number of wounded marriages, if they go untreated, may in time experience an affair involving a third party. Obviously, this adds to the pain if discovered.

An extramarital affair throws a wounded marriage into a downward spiral from which recovery may not be possible. It is often the final straw that breaks the back of the marriage relationship. Adultery is about as deadly a disease as any marriage can suffer.

The Ten Commandments trumpet God's warning, "You shall not commit adultery" (Exod. 20:14). The reason for this warning is that marriage is sacred in God's eyes and should not be violated. This commandment is for the protection of the permanent union of husband and wife as well as for the stability and foundation of the larger family.

127

An affair can be both a symptom and a cause of the dissolution of a marriage. A wounded relationship quickly becomes vulnerable to the temptations of an affair. What are the dynamics behind an affair?

A wounded marriage is one in which the couple's love and passion for each other have cooled for one reason or another. Resentment may have swelled up as a result of long-standing, unmet needs. Neglect of daily affection between the couple may have produced a distancing from each other, both psychologically and physically. Dullness and drabness in feelings for each other may have set in, possibly brought on by nothing more than the daily routine of living together and making a living.

Then the bombshell drops. The beautiful secretary or other coworker begins to look tantalizing and appealing to a man in a wounded marriage. The handsome, attentive boss or other coworker in the office may begin to attract a neglected and resentful wife in a wounded marriage.

*Pat was a math teacher in a local high school. Linda taught history in the room next to his. Both had wounded marriages. Pat's wife, Joan, was a housewife with three small children. They had been married for nine years. Their affectionate feelings for each other as well as their sex life had grown cold with disinterest, especially on Joan's part. It was a daily exhausting experience to manage three small children. At the end of the day, she felt worn out and numb. Affection and sex were her least interests. Moreover, she gave her mother more attention than she did her husband.*

*Linda's husband, George, was a professional golfer who traveled much of the time. Consequently, she would come home to an empty apartment for days on end. Life became extremely lonely and boring, mostly grading papers and watching television by herself. When George was in town, his interests were focused mainly on his fellow golfers at the local golf club and a nearby night club. Linda and George had no children, and they had been gradually drifting apart for the four years of their marriage.*

# The Affair 129

*Pat and Linda were both extremely vulnerable for an affair. Teaching in the same school, they saw a lot of each other. They began spending time together at breaks in one or the other's classroom, in the faculty lounge, in the cafeteria for lunch, and eventually in the parking lot sitting in a car just talking. His cologne and her perfume began to mingle with an unusual power of attraction. Their conversations began to center upon many commonalities that each discovered in the other.*

*In time, the sexual attraction was too much. They began to rendezvous either at a local motel or by a hidden lake outside the city. In the back of their minds they easily justified such behavior. For both of them it was a type of revenge for the neglect they felt in their own marriages. Their first sexual encounter was quickly followed by considerable guilt, but in time their consciences began to wane, and before long it no longer bothered them. Their inward rationalizations soon overruled their once-sensitive consciences. The physical and emotional euphoria they each felt canceled all initial feelings of guilt.*

Conscience has a way of slipping back into the picture, however, especially late at night after the lights are turned out and you are lying in bed staring at the ceiling with your spouse lying next to you in ignorance of what is happening. If you are a Christian, the added promptings of the Holy Spirit in your disobedient heart may enliven the conscience once again. Thank God for the convicting power of the Holy Spirit, for otherwise a wounded marriage that involves an affair on the part of one or both partners would never be healed. Dissolution and divorce would be inevitable.

If you discover that your spouse is having an extramarital affair, what can you do? First, be sure of your facts. Don't take someone else's word for it. Confront your spouse in a calm and reasonable tone of voice: "Is there someone else? Are you having an affair?" If the answer is "yes," your first temptation will be to cry, scream, yell, throw things, threaten, curse, or any number of angry outbursts. But go somewhere else to express your anger, especially if children are present in the home. Find a qualified and caring counselor or therapist to listen to your expressed feelings of anger, betrayal, despair, and hurt.

As soon as possible, get a good grip on yourself. After all, what's most important here, your feelings or your marriage? If your spouse has been unfaithful, you have every right to be upset, angry, despondent, and discouraged. But wait a minute. Have a firm talk with yourself: "Maybe I contributed in some way to this situation. Where did I go wrong? In what way did I fail to live up to his or her expectations of me? What marital needs did I not meet?"

In most affairs, there are both *push* and *pull* factors. The attraction of the other person certainly represents part of the *pull* factors, pulling your spouse away from you. But there were probably some *push* factors in your behavior and attitudes that pushed your spouse away from you. Can you identify what those might have been? Try to recall what your spouse tended to complain most about in recent months.

Of course, I don't mean to imply that the affair is all your fault. Your spouse may simply be promiscuous, with few, if any, moral values regarding marriage. There is very little you can do about that. Your spouse may think of *love* as merely sexual, and the physical element may be the predominant drive in the affair. Sex at home may have become routine and without feeling or intimacy, so he or she has looked for a thrill elsewhere. The inevitable guilt about the unfaithfulness turns into a blaming of you for the failed marriage.

So what can you do? After being sure of your facts, you will need to decide whether your marriage is worth saving or not. If you are a Christian, I believe that you are obligated to try to save your marriage. Jesus did say that divorce is justified if there is "marital unfaithfulness" (Matt. 19:9), but he also taught about unlimited forgiveness

# The Affair 131

toward those who offend us (see Matt. 18:21–35). The apostle Paul enjoined us to forgive "each other, just as in Christ God forgave you" (Eph. 4:32). There is also that magnanimous story in the Old Testament about God telling the prophet Hosea to take back his adulterous wife, Gomer, based upon the example of God himself taking back his adulterous people, Israel.

If you decide your marriage is worth saving, then ask your spouse to sit down with you (just the two of you) and talk about what is at stake. You will need to not only forgive your spouse but also ask for forgiveness for your own shortcomings in the relationship; the faults are not likely to be one-sided. This is where an honest look at yourself is going to be absolutely essential for healing the rupture.

Tell your spouse, "Let's both go and get some help from a competent marriage counselor. I suppose that we both need help, but I can only speak for myself. Please help me get the kind of assistance I need to be the spouse I was for you when we first got married, but more than that, to be the spouse you need and want now. For whatever you have done, I forgive you. Yet I need you to forgive me for my failures as well. Together, we can work this out." Major on using *I* messages rather than *you* messages. Any attempts to accuse or blame the other (*you* messages) will quickly drive the relationship toward eventual failure. Reconciliation never travels with condemnation.

Your spouse may say, "No, it's too late," and that will be the end of that. But at least you will be doing everything within your ability to reverse the situation. In more cases than not, you will not be able to save the marriage by yourself. You will need God's help, you will need the help of supportive friends and relatives, and you will need the help of a competent marriage counselor or therapist. Chapter 23 will discuss how to find such a person. Whatever you do, don't try to cope alone.

You may think your marriage is dead when you learn of the affair, but the central message of the Bible is that there is life after death. The God revealed in Jesus Christ is the God of resurrection. He can raise a dead marriage back to life. You can survive infidelity.[38]

# 21

## The Divorce

Some wounded marriages will end in divorce. For some couples, a divorce is both painful and a great relief. So much damage has been done that the pain experienced in the final decree is mingled with a sense of relief. Yet regardless of the feeling of relief that "it's finally over," there is often a lingering of trauma, the pain of failure, and the hurt of shattered dreams. If there are children to consider, the pain spreads to them and hangs over their heads like a dark cloud.

Children of divorce often feel that the dissolution of their parents' marriage was somehow their fault. A child may even actually say, "Mommy/Daddy, what did I do or say that made you want to divorce? How did I come between you two? Whatever it was, please forgive me!" Children of divorce will remember the arguments their parents had over them. They will conclude, usually erroneously, that they were somehow to blame. So a part of the pain of divorce is watching your children bear this false guilt. It would be important for you to take such children to a competent family therapist to help them work through these false guilt feelings. Otherwise they may be emotionally crippled for years to come.

## The What-If Game

Couples who end up in divorce often play certain mental games in an attempt to cope with their emotions. One such mental exercise is the *what-if game*. After the divorce there will be a strong temptation to survey the past years and punish yourself with such thoughts as:

What if I had been a better wife (or husband)?

What if we had not moved to this new job or to this particular city?

What if I had not allowed my mother (or father) to interfere with our marriage?

What if I had not gone to work but had stayed home with the children?

What if I had been more affirming, more sexual, more generous, more affectionate, less complaining, less nagging, less negative, more positive, etc?

What if we had gone to church more faithfully?

The "what ifs" can be endless. Such questions are not only a form of self-flagellation but also are nonproductive and a waste of mental and emotional energy. Such mental gymnastics and searching go nowhere. This game is a self-imposed guilt trip; you are assuming full responsibility for what happened. True, you may be partially responsible in some ways, but about all you can do now is to recognize those mistakes, confess them to God and, if possible, to your ex-spouse, and get on with your life.

# The Divorce

How do you confess your perceived mistakes? The Bible has much to say about confession, pertaining both to confession to God and to others (see Ps. 32; Prov. 28:13; Matt. 5:23–24; James 5:16; 1 John 1:9). God's forgiveness is clearly promised and eagerly offered. Confessing to your ex-spouse will be difficult and even doubted as sincere. Maybe your only choice is to write a letter using *I* messages and not *you* messages. Yet, however received, there is healing and therapeutic power in confession.

## The Blame Game

Another mental game a divorced person may play is the *blame game*. Your first temptation with this game will be to blame your ex-spouse:

It was all his (or her) fault.

I was the good spouse.

I was the one who worked the hardest to save the marriage.

I was the loving, affectionate, responsible one.

My Ex was insensitive, uncaring, unaffectionate, irresponsible, immoral, and did not meet my needs.

The blame game is psychologically designed to make you feel righteous, imposed upon, mistreated, abused, and guiltless. This game is a subconscious effort to defend, protect, and cover up a wounded ego. But deep down inside, you probably know that you really can't place all the blame on your Ex. You have to bear at least some, if not a lot, of the responsibility for what happened. If both of you play the blame game, it won't be long before you realize that no one wins this game. It is extremely counterproductive and a no-win situation for both of you.

Whatever you do, don't continue to criticize, run down, or castigate your ex-spouse to your children. Your Ex is still their father or mother. In most cases, they love you both dearly. You subject them to a great deal of suffering when you try to make your Ex look like the bad person in your former marriage. Your children will probably deeply resent your continuing these verbal expressions of your deep-seated anger toward your Ex, and it could eventually cause them to pull away from you. What child, younger or older, wants to hear his or her father or mother dragged through the mud all the time? Before your children, always speak respectfully of their other parent. You never win when you speak disrespectfully of another.

## Biblical Grounds

Sometimes a divorce may be justified. Where there is blatant infidelity and an unwillingness to repent and seek forgiveness on the part of your spouse, where there is consistent physical and emotional abuse, or where there is abandonment, divorce may be justified. Each case must be examined and evaluated on its own individual elements. Read Matthew 19:1–12 and 1 Corinthians 7 carefully and discuss your situation with a wise pastoral counselor. Also, remember that the biblical texts do not address all the different possible case scenarios of failed marriages. A careful reader of the Bible must work from biblical principles regarding such a delicate subject as divorce.

## Reconciliation

Although it is rare, sometimes a divorce is not the end of a marriage. With the vast array of Christian resources, gen-

# The Divorce 137

uine reconciliation is a possibility. I have known several divorced couples who found good counseling help and eventually remarried each other. Most of the time, these situations involved a couple who were not Christians but who, after their divorce, invited Jesus Christ into their lives. With this new relationship to God and with a totally new perspective on life, they reconciled and started over.

What made the difference? The apostle Paul expressed it best when he wrote, "Therefore, if anyone is in Christ, he is a new creation; the old has gone, the new has come! All this is from God, who reconciled us to himself through Christ and gave us the ministry of reconciliation" (2 Cor. 5:17–18). When we are reconciled to God, we gain the resources and strength to become reconciled to one another—yes, even to an ex-spouse.

*Fay and David had been married almost fifteen years and had two children when they divorced. Their married life was a mix of ups and downs, goods and bads, happiness and unhappiness, peace and conflict. As the years rolled by, they became very stressed-out people—over their jobs, their children, their interfering relatives, spending too much money, drinking too much, and an overscheduled lifestyle.*

*They had been somewhat involved in church during their teen and college years, but they later allowed marriage, family, and vocational ambition to bring that to a halt. In time, Fay discovered that David was involved in a couple of brief extramarital affairs. She never really forgave him. He tried to justify his behavior. Arguments increased to the point that being in the same house was miserable for everyone, including the children. Divorce was inevitable.*

*Following the divorce, David went into a deep depression. He felt that his life was one big blank—a miserable failure. He finally admitted to himself that he was an extremely unhappy man, and it was no one else's fault but his own. He went on a business trip one week, and in the motel where he was staying he opened the drawer of the bedside table and found a Gideon Bible. Call it what you will—curiosity, divine providence—he began to read. In the front section of the Bible there were guidelines for reading the Bible. Some of the topics intrigued him because he identified with them: depression, despondency, failure, etc. The suggested verses spoke to him like dynamite, exploding his sense of self-sufficiency and self-righteousness. The verses pointing to how to become a Christian opened his eyes to his greatest need: a right relationship with God.*

*David fell on his knees by the bed and prayed as he had never prayed before. Oh, he had said prayers from time to time in past years, but either in a formal context (before a family meal) or in some foxhole experience of financial desperation. But this night his prayer was different. He confessed his sins to God, including his sins as a failed and unfaithful husband, and claimed God's forgiveness. He asked the Lord Jesus Christ to come into his life and take over, including his personality, his desires, his life goals, his physical needs, his job, as well as his failed marriage if there was any hope of reconciliation with Fay.*

*When he returned from that trip, David sought out a pastor recommended by a close business associate. For several days they talked about what this new commitment could mean to David and possibly even to Fay. David called Fay and asked to take her to lunch. When he told her what had happened, she could tell he was different, but she was naturally skeptical. In time, David was able to share with Fay what he had discovered in the Bible. He wisely did so in a nonjudgmental manner. He shared simply as a witness: "This is what happened to me." Fay began visiting with the same pastor who had counseled David. After a few weeks, Fay and David both publicly confessed Christ in the pastor's church. In a couple of months, they decided to remarry.*

*David and Fay did not find a spiritual quick fix. Their pastor walked slowly with them, both individually and together, through the mistakes and pain of their failed marriage. This wise counseling continued for several months even after their remarriage. Some of the old relational barnacles had to be knocked off of their personalities. Some old scars remained, but genuine healing was taking place in their relationship. With Christ as their new Savior and Lord, they had a new dynamic and motivation to make their marriage work. They*

# The Divorce 139

*discovered with the apostle Paul the truth of his own testimony, "I can do all things through Him [Christ] who strengthens me" (Phil. 4:13 NASB).*

Most divorced couples will not be so fortunate as David and Fay. There will have been too much damage and an unwillingness on the part of one or both to seek reconciliation. Most divorced persons will remarry someone else in time. If that is your experience, you can still find a new and meaningful, redemptive relationship with God. With God's help and the instrumental assistance of a good counselor, try to discover what elements contributed to your divorce, especially those factors for which you must take a measure of responsibility. If you don't understand something of what produced the failure of your prior marriage, you may be doomed to repeat those mistakes again. And you certainly don't want to do that. Learn from your mistakes.

# 22

# The Reconciliation

It is possible for a wounded marriage to experience genuine reconciliation. To reconcile means to restore to friendship or harmony, to settle or resolve differences, to bring peace between two separated, even warring, parties. The case of David and Fay in the previous chapter dealt with a divorced couple who remarried. This chapter will focus on wounded marriages that do not divorce but come to grips with their conflicts and differences and resolve them in peaceful harmony before ever reaching the divorce stage.

The idea of a wounded marriage implies some degree of emotional and relational separation but not necessarily geographic or physical separation. If a marriage is wounded, it suggests that a serious degree of distancing between the couple has taken place over a period of time. Most wounded couples are not aware of the specific dynamics that have contributed to the emotional and relational distancing. They are so close to the reality that they do not understand what has happened to them.

Reconciliation calls for both husband and wife to face up to the reality of their situation—facing the facts of what has happened to the marriage since the wedding day. Whether few or many, the years have passed by and certain changes have taken place in the relationship. Even with as few as five or ten years into marriage, you are not exactly the same person you were at the beginning. Changes—including physical, medical, emotional, mental, vocational, and attitudinal—can have a considerable impact on a marriage. These changes can produce either good or bad consequences in the marriage depending on how the couple responds to them. Some people don't respond to change very well, so a change that might strengthen one marriage could have a deleterious effect on another. As examples, a sizable increase in income could impact a marriage either negatively or positively, or a serious medical problem could either strengthen or weaken a marriage, depending on the couple's response.

A reality check of your marriage requires an honest appraisal of the changes that have come along the way. There are changes that result from growing older. If you married in your early twenties and have been married ten years, you are now in your early thirties, and that means you look, think, feel, and act differently whether you recognize it or not. Since both of you are ten years older, you may not be responding well to these changes.

During the prior years of marriage, you have gone through other transitions that might include: increased education, job promotions, job losses or demotions, the birth of children, moves to new locations, emerging conflicts with relatives and friends, financial mismanagement either at home or in your business, a cooling of romantic interest in your spouse, or any number of possible traumas (e.g., a car wreck, a miscarriage, a debilitating illness, postpartum depression, unexpected deaths of close relatives, an IRS audit, having your home burglarized).

# The Reconciliation 143

Such changes may have negatively impacted your marriage, and it is important to realize that the stress they have brought to your relationship does not necessarily mean that you no longer love each other. Your marital woundedness may not mean that you have a weak or poor marriage but rather that you need to improve and strengthen your coping skills in dealing with change. One way to upgrade your coping skills is to participate in a wounded marriage support group. Persons in similar situations, properly led by a qualified facilitator, can greatly assist a wounded couple to work through the impact of the above-mentioned changes toward meaningful reconciliation.

An excellent resource for assisting in the establishment of such a support group has been compiled by Johnny Jones, *Life Support Leader's Handbook: Your Church's Lifeline to Hurting People.*[39] This handbook includes an administrative guide for conducting Christ-centered support group ministries, descriptions of various psychological and relational problems that can be addressed by support groups, criteria for selecting discovery group leaders and support group facilitators, helps for training both new and experienced leaders, descriptions of group dynamics, specific helps for guiding effective group experiences, guidance for making referrals to trained counselors, ideas for promoting support group ministries in the community, and strategies for enlisting participants.

Also, a wounded marriage support group could use this book as a background reader. The list of discussion questions found at the end of the book can be used by facilitators of such a group. The group could meet for thirteen weeks (three months), reading and discussing two chapters per week. The first session would be an organizational meeting to lay down ground rules for the group's meetings and discussions. The last session would be a summary and wrap-up for the three months of meetings, possibly making plans to reach out to other wounded couples with subsequent support groups.

As valuable as a support group might be to you, the bottom line for reconciliation will be the hard work you and your spouse will do by yourselves, at home, in the privacy of your own intimate relationship. In order to experience reconciliation in a wounded marriage, it is vital to

- learn to recognize the stressors in your marriage (the reality check).
- learn how to cope with the ongoing changes in your lives.
- learn how to be sensitive and understanding regarding the feelings of your spouse.
- learn how to be forgiving of your spouse's mistakes.
- learn how to be open and honest in confessing your own mistakes.
- learn how to laugh again, to play, to enjoy, and to celebrate life as it is lived out day by day.

However, it is also extremely important to recognize that reconciliation is not a one-time experience. It is an ongoing attitude, a frame of mind, a way of thinking and relating, which are the results of a maturing love relationship between a husband and wife.

*Roy and Anita learned to develop the spirit of reconciliation in their marriage. Having married in their early twenties right out of college, they quickly had three children before they reached thirty years of age. Roy was a workaholic, spending very little time at home with the family, trying to get his career into high gear. After seven years of marriage, Anita finally had enough of being an abandoned wife and raising the children by herself. At first Roy resisted Anita's efforts to get him to cut back his hours at work so he could spend time with the family.*

*Since arguing did little good, Anita finally took the children and moved home with her parents. This awakened Roy to the realization that his wife was serious. With the help of a competent marriage*

# The Reconciliation 145

*counselor, Roy and Anita agreed to a compromise to meet in the middle between Roy's career and Anita's need for her children to have a father at home.*

*In their late thirties, Roy and Anita faced a crisis with their then rebellious and stubborn teenage children. These new problems drove them to seek help from a local church and its pastor. Just as the stress on their marriage had reached a breaking point, they became Christians, which bound them together with a common spiritual experience. Instead of turning on each other as they had many times before, they now pulled together with their common bond in Christ. This was no quick fix for their parent-teen problems, but at least they now had new resources for coping.*

*In their midforties, Roy and Anita experienced new stresses over their elderly and somewhat dependent parents. The original parent-child roles were now reversed. Sharp and ugly disagreements developed over how to relate to their parents. In addition, Roy felt Anita was pulling away from him to care for her parents. When Anita learned that Roy was strongly attracted to his young secretary (but short of an affair), the marriage experienced woundedness again. By this age, Roy and Anita were learning the value of open and honest confrontation and communication regarding marital stress. A support group in their church helped them to rise above these problems and arrive at some sensible solutions.*

*During their fifties, Roy and Anita went through the grieving process surrounding the deaths of their parents as well as the pain related to the divorce of their oldest son and his wife. Instead of turning on each other in frustration, as they had in their earlier years, they now turned to each other for mutual support and encouragement. They had learned to live a reconciled lifestyle with an attitude of working things through rather than allowing life's stresses to pull them apart.*

Roy and Anita grew to engage in an ongoing ministry of reconciliation within their marriage. Even though life-cycle changes may bring wounds to a marriage, an entrenched spirit of reconciliation can heal those wounds as a husband and wife become wounded healers to one another.

# 23

# The Counselor

Couples in a wounded marriage would be wise to seek out a competent marriage counselor. However, a good marriage counselor will not offer a relational panacea or a marital cure-all because such persons only offer their skills to facilitate a couple's active engagement in the healing process. There is simply no guarantee that a marriage counselor can bring healing to a wounded marriage. However, without a competent counselor, it is very unlikely that a wounded marriage will experience the healing it needs.

## Reticence to Seek Counseling

One major problem exists with many wounded couples who need to seek counseling: One or both are either afraid or too proud to admit their problem and seek help. They don't want their relatives, friends, or work associates to discover that they have a problem. Even wounded couples want others to think the best of them—that all is well with their marriage. This is especially true of religiously prominent people, such as pastors, deacons, elders, Sunday school teachers, church staff ministers, seminary students, missionaries, or other denominational employees.

Strange but true, in our culture it is acceptable to admit that you have a physical or medical problem but not a marital difficulty. For some unexplainable reason, contemporary church culture considers a marital problem as evidence of a major moral or spiritual defect. This cultural ideology teaches that good Christian people will never have a wounded marriage. Dedicated Christians are supposed to be immune to such difficulties.

My answer to that is simple: "baloney." Christians don't wear an *S* or a *W* on their undershirts. There are no Superman Christian husbands or Wonderwoman Christian wives. Even the most godly Christians are susceptible to relational problems. A reading of church history reveals that some of the great figures in the life of the Christian church had very poor marriages:

Methodism's founder, John Wesley, married a widow, Molly Vazeille, and it was not a good marriage. They eventually separated.

Scottish missionary David Livingstone's marriage to Mary Moffat was a virtual disaster, partly because he was gone from her so much of the time in his travels.

Being a Christian ought to provide motivation and good sense to seek help for whatever problems you have. Denial of marital difficulties is no virtue in the Christian faith. If you are afraid to seek counseling for fear of exposure to peers and the public, what will you say to them if the marriage finally falls apart for lack of help? As for being too proud to seek help, the Bible says, "Pride goes before destruction, a

# The Counselor

haughty spirit before a fall" (Prov. 16:18). If you broke your leg, would you be too proud to seek a medical doctor's assistance? Isn't your marriage more important than your bones?

## Finding a Counselor

How do you find a competent and qualified marriage counselor? You need to know that there are some quacks who are competing in the marriage counseling market. These unqualified persons have very dubious credentials. Simply because they may call themselves "Doctor" does not mean they are academically and clinically trained. In many states it is possible for anyone to hang out a shingle marked "Marriage and Family Counselor" with almost no qualifications for engaging in such a practice. Fortunately, a growing number of states have passed legislation requiring counselors to be certified and/or licensed based upon academic degrees and examination. However, this often applies only to those who call themselves a "psychologist" rather than "marriage and family counselor." So you have to be careful in shopping around for someone qualified.

I recommend that you start with the pastor of your church or a pastor you may know. A few pastors have C.P.E. (Clinical Pastoral Education) certification or some similar clinical training in professional counseling. These persons have several hundred hours of supervised clinical counseling experience, and they usually make excellent marriage counselors. If your pastor is not so qualified, he should know where good counseling can be found and be able to refer you to someone capable.

Most competent private practice counselors can be detected by their professional affiliations. In their yellow pages telephone listing you may notice those who are affiliated with The American Association of Pastoral Counselors (AAPC) and The American Association of Marriage and Family Therapists (AAMFT). Some social workers who have the Master of Social Work degree (M.S.W.) are also members of the Academy of Certified Social Workers (ACSW), indicating they have special training in marriage counseling.

Some marriage counselors received their training in the field of psychology with a masters degree (M.A. or M.S.) or the Doctor of Philosophy degree (Ph.D.). If they list themselves as a Licensed Psychologist, this means they have passed the board examinations for their state, which are regulated by law. They are often referred to as "clinical psychologists."

University schools of education and schools of home economics may also offer special counseling degrees, and these graduates may list themselves as marriage counselors (M.A., M.Ed., Ed.D., or Ph.D. degrees). They may or may not have had clinical supervision in marriage counseling—it pays to ask.

Many states now require private practice counselors to be licensed by meeting certain high standards. They will list their name in the phone book as an "L.P.C." (Licensed Professional Counselor). This has helped to eliminate unqualified counselors from advertising and practicing.

Be careful regarding a counselor's advertised academic degree listings. Some listings of Ph.D. or other doctoral degrees may be bogus. I once discovered a counselor who worked out of her home and advertised herself with an M.Ed. (Master of Education degree) with a major in school counseling and guidance and a Ph.D. in biblical counseling from an unaccredited "theological degree mill" in California that is widely known for its bogus degrees. She had no official license or certification from any state agency or reputable certifying association. When one of my church members told me what kind of counseling advice this woman was giving

# The Counselor

his wife, I quickly recognized her skills as dubious if not dangerous.

Some medical doctors (M.D.) are trained through a psychiatric residency program in marriage counseling. Not all psychiatrists are so trained, but some are.

Actually, one of the best referral sources for finding good marriage counselors will be your family doctor, especially if he or she has a family practice specialty. And it just may be that some of your marital problems are medically or physiologically related and call for the consultation of a medical doctor in consort with a professional marriage counselor. As a pastoral marriage counselor, I have often worked with the couple's family physician or other medical specialist when some of their problems needed medical advice or treatment.

A growing number of persons with pastoral experience and who earned the M.Div. (Master of Divinity) degree have subsequently earned the D.Min. (Doctor of Ministry) degree and are engaging in professional marriage counseling. If their D.Min. degree was earned in an accredited graduate divinity school where the major was in marriage and family counseling followed by clinical supervision, then they may well be qualified. But most who hold the D.Min. degree are not so qualified, so be discriminating and ask about their training. In most states, pastoral counselors working under the sponsorship of a church are not required by law to be licensed by the state as an L.P.C.

What about the cost of marriage counseling? Reputable counselors will be up-front with you about their fees. Many are physician affiliated and can work with your medical insurance coverage. Some, especially those who counsel in a community or church-supported agency, use a sliding scale fee based on your income or ability to pay. But whatever the cost, it will be much cheaper than the expense of a divorce. Ask anyone who has been through it. Yet think of the greater

## Be Prepared

Now I must advise you about four very important factors to be faced in marriage counseling:

1. *It will be hard work for both you and your spouse.* Serious counseling is never easy because it is so much more than just listening to wise advice from the counselor. Actually, a competent counselor will go slow on advice and will seek to guide you to make your own decisions that will precipitate constructive change. A good counselor is not a quick-fix person with all the answers to your problems. Rather, he or she is a guide to help you clarify the best solutions from the available alternatives.

2. *Constructive marriage counseling will take time.* You will probably need to meet once a week for several months or more. Be patient. Your marital injuries didn't happen overnight, and neither will healing take place quickly. Apply yourself diligently and patiently to make the necessary changes in your marriage.

3. *Be prepared for your own personality structure and behavior patterns to vigorously resist change.* Because personality and behavioral changes are frightening to many hurting people, the thought of change causes a swelling of inner resistance. If you are naturally *externally oriented* regarding the nature of your marital problems (that is, the cause is always out there; it is someone else's fault, not yours, and changes must be made by the other person), then any suggestion that you need to change will be aggressively opposed by your inner psyche. However, if you can learn to be *internally oriented* regarding your marriage difficulties (that is, many of the roots of the problem lie within yourself, and any

# The Counselor 153

solutions must somehow begin within your own mind, something you have control over), then there will be a greater willingness to make necessary changes.

4. *Successful marriage counseling is achieved by those who initially set the goal of success.* If your marriage is of utmost value to you, instead of having the attitude, "Well, I'll give this a try," you will be motivated to stay with the counseling process and determine to grow through it to become a better husband or wife and to heal the woundedness of your marriage.

I have observed that a large number of people who refuse to engage in the healing work of restoring a wounded marriage and end up in divorce never really learned why the failure took place, never made any significant personality and relational changes, and then tended to repeat their woundedness in a subsequent marriage. You really don't want to do that!

Good marriage counseling is available. Learn how to find it. Inquire and shop around. Cooperate with your therapist. Do it together. Work hard at it. Spend the necessary time and money. Be patient. Don't let occasional reversals throw you. Assume your share of the responsibility for making changes. Be open to change and don't fight it. And, remember, you don't have to do this alone—God wants to help you. Ask him.

To seek competent marriage counseling at this time in your life may well be one of the most significant decisions you will ever make.

# 24

# The Healing

It has been the purpose of this book to guide the readers—persons with wounded marriages—to engage in the healing process. Modern medical knowledge of the human body tells us that most of the time the body heals itself of most injuries and illnesses. The body has been so designed by the Creator that there are recuperative powers within it to fend off germs, viruses, and infections as well as heal broken bones, bruises, and other physical injuries. However, sometimes these problems are so severe that they overwhelm the body's natural capacity to heal itself, and the intervention of medical treatment is required.

To some degree the marital relationship is very similar to the physical body. Most of the time, marriages can handle the day-to-day bumps, bruises, cuts, injuries, and relational toxicities of living together. A couple's love for and commitment to each other provide natural recuperative powers, a kind of relational immune system, to keep the marriage healthy and functioning in desirable and pleasurable ways.

156 Re-Igniting Love and Passion

However, many married couples find themselves experiencing far beyond the usual amount of stresses and strains of daily living. Over a period of time, they become wounded. The hurt doesn't heal naturally or quickly. A wake-up call is needed. Some form of direct intervention is called for. Radical action is required. Without healing, marital death will ensue.

For clarification, let me repeat the definition of a wounded marriage: An intact marriage of variable length wherein one or, more likely, both partners experience a serious degree of emotional pain resulting from accumulating disappointments and discouragements in the relationship. Even reasonable expectations have not been met, and it appears that they never will be if the relationship continues on its present course. In addition, complementary needs are not being met satisfactorily, including physical, relational, emotional, mental, and spiritual needs.

Characteristics and symptoms of a wounded marriage may include: emotional pain, anger, rage, depression, infidelity, dysfunctionality, frigidity, revenge, distance, separation, confusion, and possibly psychosomatic illnesses.

Permanent healing for a wounded marriage lies ultimately in the hands of God. Of course, many marriages work without any reference to or dependence upon God. But marriage as the divine Creator intended it, that is, as it reaches its fullest potential in love and joy, can only come as God's gift to us, and the fullness of that gift is primarily to be found in a saving, personal, and vital relationship with God revealed in his Son, Jesus Christ.

## Healing Your Marriage

This gift of a Christ-centered marriage contains within it a task: the hard work of making a marriage succeed. Several

# The Healing 157

suggestions related to this task can assist in healing a wounded marriage:

1. *Recognize the difference between reality and fantasy.* Every marriage has its painful moments, its serious disappointments, and its discouraging situations. This is life, and as psychiatrist M. Scott Peck says, "Life is difficult."[40] Most marriages are not going to be lived out in a warm and comfortable cottage with a white picket fence in a peaceful country meadow. Such expectations are fantasy. Reality includes dishes, diapers, debts, discouragements, disease, and death, as well as joy, pleasure, fun, happiness, comfort, births, health, and warm fuzzies. We need to be prepared when life enrolls us in the University of Hard Knocks. Growth is wonderful, but there are always growing pains.

2. *Learn to lower your overly idealized expectations.* Otherwise you are setting yourself up to be hurt. Expect the inevitable imperfections of your spouse as well as the day-to-day routine of your marriage. It's great to set worthy goals for a marriage, but don't forget your common humanity. Nothing is perfect in this life, and that includes your marriage.

3. *Stop trying to change your spouse and start working on changing yourself.* You are the only one you can really do anything about. If both marriage partners do this, then the obvious result will be constructive changes in both of you. If you begin by trying to change your spouse, expect a heavy dose of resistance. This is human nature. Focus on *you*—the changes you need to make—and watch the ripple effect of change in those about you.

4. *Identify your spouse's needs and concentrate on meeting them in specific and concrete ways.* Go back and reread chapter 4, The Needs. Again, if both marriage partners do this, then the obvious result will be that both of you will be getting your needs met. Yet the focus here is on giving, not on getting. If you both give, you will both get. However, if you are only concerned about getting your own needs met, your

selfishness will destroy the complementary meeting of each other's needs. Jesus' Golden Rule certainly applies here: "So in everything, do to others what you would have them do to you, for this sums up the Law and the Prophets" (Matt. 7:12).

5. *Discover the nature of the unfinished business of your childhood and do something about it.* Stop blaming your spouse for what one of your parents did or didn't do to or for you. Only you can resolve the problems of your past. If you expect your marriage to do that, you may well overload its relational circuits. You can best resolve the difficulties out of your past that you brought into your marriage through competent counseling assistance, which is the next point.

6. *Secure qualified professional counseling both as an individual and as a couple.* Make your goal to

- understand, take charge of, and resolve that part of your past that continues to dominate your present.
- learn how to take charge of your emotions.
- learn effective coping skills.
- learn better communication skills.
- discover how to improve your self-image and raise your self-esteem.
- stimulate permanent change in yourself.

7. *Consider organizing and participating in an ongoing small support group that focuses on the healing of wounded marriages.* Make certain that your group is competently led by a qualified person.

8. *Engage in occasional marriage enrichment retreats and take advantage of published resources on marriage enrichment.* Ask the pastor of your local church to assist you as a resource person in both of these opportunities.

9. *Focus on a spiritual renewal in your own life.* Commit yourself, preferably as a couple, to begin a process of spiritual growth by means of the classic disciplines (prayer, wor-

# The Healing 159

ship, devotional and systematic Bible reading, meditation, contemplation, and sharing your faith) for deepening your relationship with God.[41] Many wounded marriages have at their very heart a spiritual problem. They have a *God problem*, and only God can solve such a problem.

## Forgiveness

The ultimate balm for healing a wounded marriage is forgiveness. Without it, there will be no healing. But you may be asking, "How do I forgive someone who has hurt me so much and so often?" Well, you have to experience forgiveness yourself, and the best place to do this is in the presence of Jesus Christ, who died on the cross for your sins. This was the apostle Paul's advice to all of us: "Be kind and compassionate to one another, forgiving each other, just as in Christ God forgave you" (Eph. 4:32). So if you want to learn how to forgive, you have to be forgiven yourself. Once you have experienced God's forgiveness in Christ, then you have the resources to forgive your spouse for whatever he or she has done to you.

You say, "But that hurts! It's so painful forgiving him (or her) for what happened." Yes, just as it must have been extremely painful when Jesus Christ was nailed to that cross to die. Forgiveness always carries the pain of sacrificial love. You cannot do this in your own strength. Only a *new you* can do this—the new person in Christ that God wants you to be.

God has a new you waiting to be discovered. And when both you and your spouse have made this discovery, a new marriage awaits both of you.

When God heals a wounded marriage, he isn't going to iron out all of your marital wrinkles, solve all of your relational problems, and immediately take away all the pain inflicted in the past. The reason is that he wants you both to remember who healed you so that he can continue to heal you when future injuries come. But there is a broader purpose: God also wants you both to become *wounded healers* of other wounded marriages, because your marriage should not be an end in itself. God intends your marriage to be a means of ministry and mission to other hurting people. In a very real sense, your healing can become the balm in the healing of others.

God is offering you healing for your wounded marriage. Now go for it!

# Questions for Discussion in a Support Group

These questions are arranged for use in a thirteen-week support group for wounded marriages. Each session should last approximately two hours in an informal and comfortable setting. A qualified facilitator who is thoroughly familiar with the material in the book should lead each session. See chapter 22 for resources and suggestions in organizing and leading a support group.

One important question will need to be faced from the very beginning: Should participants attend as couples or as individuals? This is difficult to answer. It all depends on the persons involved. Obviously, some might not feel free to express themselves with their spouse present. One solution would be to have two separate groups with separate facilitators, one for wives and another for husbands, meeting in nearby locations for convenience sake. One ground rule is an absolute must: confidentiality regarding whatever is shared in the group.

It will be very important for participants to read the chapters to be discussed *before* coming to that particular session. One exception might be the first session when some participants will have just received their copy of the book. The facilitator may briefly summarize chapter 1 after the introductions of participants. At the end of each session the facilitator should remind the participants of the reading assignment for the next session.

161

## 162 Questions for Discussion in a Support Group

### *Session 1* Introduction, The Pain: Chapter 1

1. Tell us who you are, when and where you were married, how long you have been married, and what you hope to accomplish from this group experience.
2. Briefly describe the three major problems in your marriage.
3. What feelings do you have when you talk about these three problems? What words did you circle in the list in chapter 1, pages 13–14 ?
4. What are some positive functions of the emotional pain experienced in a wounded marriage? What are some negative functions of this pain?

### *Session 2* The Honeymoon, The Expectations: Chapters 2 and 3

1. What happened on your honeymoon, both positive and negative? What feelings do these memories bring?
2. What revelations did you have on your honeymoon regarding your spouse? What changes have taken place since then?
3. What three major expectations did you bring to your marriage? If they were not met, tell us how you feel about that.
4. What was it that you always wanted your parent of the opposite sex to say to you that he or she never said? How do you feel about that? Have you transferred these expectations to your spouse? What has been the result?

### *Session 3* The Needs, The Conflict: Chapters 4 and 5

1. What primary needs did you bring to your marriage? To what degree have these been met or not met?

# Questions for Discussion in a Support Group 163

2. Did Dr. Harley's lists of needs help you identify your needs and those of your spouse? Personalize these needs as they apply to your marriage.
3. Over what do you and your spouse tend to have conflict? How do you handle conflict?
4. How would you compare the use of *I* messages with *you* messages in resolving conflict? One couple in the group might be willing to role-play this difference.

### *Session 4* The Words, The Anger: Chapters 6 and 7

1. What words does your spouse use that hurt you the most? Is this hurt simply unavoidable or a chosen response?
2. What recent examples can you think of in a conversation with your spouse when you said something you did not mean? How would you now analyze what you said?
3. What are some of the possible dynamics behind expressions of marital anger?
4. Which theory of anger do you most identify with? Give examples of anger in your marriage (and possibly how it could be used as revenge/punishment or defense/protection). Do you agree that all emotions are chosen responses?

### *Session 5* The Fears, The Tears: Chapters 8 and 9

1. What fears do you experience in your marriage?
2. What would be some constructive uses of fear in a marriage relationship?
3. Do you cry much? Related to your marriage, what do you cry about most? What different kinds of tears are there?
4. What are some positive functions of shedding tears and thereby expressing your feelings? Is it okay for men to cry?

## Session 6 The Denials, The Bedroom: Chapters 10 and 11

1. Are you currently in denial? If so, what about?
2. What are some of the dangers of denial?
3. Are sexual problems the cause or the consequence of a conflicted marriage?
4. What are the major dynamics observed in the bedroom situations of Don and Amy, Rob and Alice, Jerold and Louise? What lessons do these cases suggest to you?

## Session 7 The Children, The Relatives: Chapters 12 and 13

1. Are your children a focal point of conflict in your marriage? If so, why and how? How can childless couples be wounded?
2. Are wounded parents likely to have a wounded marriage? If so, what are the dynamics at work there?
3. Have any relatives been a major factor in your wounded marriage? If so, what happened?
4. What control do we have over wounding relatives? This could be role-played by a couple in the group.

## Session 8 The Job, The Finances: Chapters 14 and 15

1. How does your work outside the home affect your marriage? What stresses do you experience?
2. How do you keep your job in a servant role rather than a master role?
3. Do you and your spouse have different family backgrounds regarding spending and saving? If so, how do you deal with these differences?
4. How can family finances become a blessing rather than a curse?

# Questions for Discussion in a Support Group 165

## *Session 9* The Church, The Bible: Chapters 16 and 17

1. Has the church been a contributing factor in your wounded marriage? If so, how?
2. Which do you and your spouse follow: the dominance/submission motif or the mutual servanthood model? If your spouse is not a Christian and you are, how are you dealing with it?
3. Have any biblical texts created a problem for your marriage? If so, which ones, and why are they a problem?
4. Did you identify with Joe's and Mary Lou's experience with the Bible? How?

## *Session 10* The Stress, The Doctor: Chapters 18 and 19

1. What are the major stress points in your marriage? What social or cultural conditions cause you stress?
2. What suggestions in chapter 18 have helped you the most in coping with stress? Discuss Jeanne Anselmo's suggestions in the group. Which seem most helpful?
3. How has your family doctor helped you regarding your marriage situation as related to medical problems?
4. Do you need a referral to a medical specialist for a specific problem? If so, ask the group members to tell you about the doctors they have found helpful.

## *Session 11* The Affair, The Divorce: Chapters 20 and 21

1. What motivates people to have an extramarital affair? How can this be prevented?
2. What are some possible *push* and *pull* factors in an affair? What are some constructive suggestions in dealing with a spouse who is having an affair?
3. What are the dynamics involved in the what-if and the blame games in coping with divorce?

166 Questions for Discussion in a Support Group

4. What was your response to the dynamics involved in the case of Fay and David? Can there be life after divorce?

### *Session 12* The Reconciliation, The Counselor: Chapters 22 and 23

1. What major changes have taken place in the marriage since your wedding day? What does a reality check tell you about your marriage?
2. What lessons did you learn from the case of Roy and Anita that could help your marriage maintain a reconciliation attitude? How has this support group helped you move toward reconciliation?
3. What are the major problems most people face when they consider going to a marriage counselor?
4. How would you go about finding a competent marriage counselor in your city or county?

### *Session 13* Summary and Closure, The Healing: Chapter 24

1. What does the *healing* of a wounded marriage mean to you? What is the ultimate source of healing for a wounded marriage? How do you get in touch with that source?
2. What is the nature of the task discovered in the gift of Christian marriage? How is spiritual growth or renewal related to this task?
3. What is the ultimate balm in the healing of a wounded marriage? Where and how do you get this balm?
4. What have been the major lessons you have learned from these thirteen sessions?
5. How can group members now become wounded healers to other wounded couples? Where do you go from here?

# Notes

## Chapter 1: The Pain

1. All names of persons in illustrations and case studies used in this book have been changed to protect their identity. Also, certain facts have been altered to guarantee anonymity.

2. See Norman Cousins, *Head First: The Biology of Hope* (New York: E. P. Dutton, 1989); Bernie S. Siegel, M.D., *Love, Medicine, and Miracles* (New York: Harper and Row, 1986); and Blair Justice, Ph.D., *Who Gets Sick: How Beliefs, Moods, and Thoughts Affect Your Health* (Los Angeles: Jeremy P. Tarcher, 1988).

## Chapter 2: The Honeymoon

3. See the interesting results of a husband and wife research team, Miriam Arond and Samuel L. Pauker, M.D., *The First Year of Marriage: What to Expect, What to Accept, and What You Can Change* (New York: Warner Books, 1987). For special treatment of the honeymoon, see pp. 218–22.

## Chapter 3: The Expectations

4. Harville Hendrix, Ph.D., *Getting the Love You Want: A Guide for Couples* (New York: Henry Holt, 1988).

5. See Maggie Scarf, *Unfinished Business: Pressure Points in the Lives of Women* (New York: Ballantine Books, 1980).

6. Hendrix, *Getting the Love You Want.*

7. Hugh Missildine, *Your Inner Child of the Past* (New York: Simon and Schuster, 1963).

## Chapter 4: The Needs

8. Willard F. Harley Jr., *His Needs, Her Needs: Building An Affair-proof Marriage* (Old Tappan, N.J.: Fleming H. Revell, 1986).

## Chapter 5: The Conflict

9. These steps are adapted from my treatment of conflict resolution in Guy Greenfield, *We Need Each Other: Reaching Deeper Levels in Our Interpersonal Relationships* (Grand Rapids: Baker Book House, 1984), 100–102.

10. Thomas Gordon, *Parent Effectiveness Training: The Tested New Way to Raise Responsible Children* (New York: Peter H. Wyden, 1970), 115–38, gives a very helpful explanation with illustrations of these two approaches in any conversation.

11. Ibid., 49–94.

## Chapter 6: The Words

12. Gordon, Parent Effectiveness Training, chaps. 6–7.

## Chapter 12: The Children

13. Rudolf Dreikurs, M.D., and Vicki Soltz, R.N., *Children: the Challenge* (New York: Hawthorn Books, 1964). These ideas are further developed by Don Dinkmeyer and Gary D. McKay, *The Parent's Handbook: Systematic Training for Effective Parenting* (Circle Pines, Minn.: American Guidance Service, 1982); see also Don Dinkmeyer et al., *The Effective Parent* (Circle Pines, Minn.: American Guidance Service, 1987).

14. See Guy Greenfield, *The Wounded Parent: Hope for Discouraged Parents*, 2d ed. (Grand Rapids: Baker Book House, 1990), especially 43–44.

15. Ibid., 65–68.

## Chapter 14: The Job

16. George Barna, *The Frog in the Kettle: What Christians Need to Know about Life in the Year 2000* (Ventura, Calif.: Regal Books, 1990), 98.

17. Cited in Gary R. Collins and Timothy E. Clinton, *Baby Boomer Blues* (Dallas: Word Publishing, 1992), 24.

18. See the excellent discussion of this problem by Wayne Oates, *Confessions of a Workaholic: The Facts about Work Addiction* (New York: World Publishing, 1971).

## Chapter 15: The Finances

19. See especially Ron Blue, *Master Your Money: A Step-by-Step Plan for Financial Freedom Revised and Updated for the Financial Realities of the 90's* (Nashville: Thomas Nelson, 1991); see also Larry Burkett, *The Complete Financial Guide for Young Couples* (Wheaton, Ill.: Victor Books, 1989); Bob Decker and Sharon Decker, *For Love and Money: Help for the Married Couple* (Nashville: Convention Press, 1991); Lee E. Davis, *5 Steps to Successful Money Management* (Nashville: Broadman Press, 1993). All of these are written by experts in the field of family finances.

# Notes 169

20. A very helpful workbook entitled *Christian Family Money Management Plan Book*, prepared by John C. Ivins, may be secured by writing to Bob E. Lynch, Stewardship Director, Baptist General Association of Virginia, P. O. Box 8568, Richmond, VA 23226. Single copies are at no charge.

## Chapter 16: The Church

21. John C. Howell, *Equality and Submission in Marriage* (Nashville: Broadman Press, 1979); see also an excellent book that goes beyond equality to servanthood written by a family-life-specialist, social-work-scholar wife and her New Testament scholar husband: Diana S. Richmond Garland and David E. Garland, *Beyond Companionship: Christians in Marriage* (Philadelphia: Westminster Press, 1986).

22. James Alsdurf and Phyllis Alsdurf, *Battered into Submission: The Tragedy of Wife Abuse in the Christian Home* (Downers Grove, Ill.: InterVarsity Press, 1989), 81–95. This Christian clinical and forensic psychologist and his wife offer a stinging indictment of the teachings of popular conference speaker Bill Gothard.

## Chapter 17: The Bible

23. G. B. Caird, *Paul's Letters from Prison*, New Clarendon Bible Series (Oxford: Oxford University Press, 1976), 78. Also, see *kephale* in Liddell and Scott's *Intermediate Greek-English Lexicon* (Oxford: Clarendon Press, 1968), 430.

24. It is always difficult for biblical literalists to come to see that, as Baptist theologian W. T. Conner often taught, "The Bible doesn't always mean what it says, but it means what it means."

25. Gordon D. Fee and Douglas Stuart, *How to Read the Bible for All Its Worth: A Guide to Understanding the Bible* (Grand Rapids: Zondervan, 1982). For an excellent discussion of sex roles in the Bible, see Gilbert Bilezikian, *Beyond Sex Roles: A Guide for the Study of Female Roles in the Bible* (Grand Rapids: Baker Book House, 1985). Even though the emphasis here is on the female, the male role is also explained.

## Chapter 18: The Stress

26. See Hans Selye, *The Stress of Life* (New York: McGraw-Hill, 1956) and *Stress Without Distress* (Philadelphia: Lippincott, 1974).

27. Jeanne Anselmo, "Dealing with Stress—Healthful Tips," edited by Pamella Editorial Services, 1991, Promotional Line #79930.

28. Dolores Curran, *Stress and the Healthy Family* (Minneapolis: Winston Press, 1985).

29. Keith W. Sehnert, M.D., *Stress/Unstress* (Minneapolis: Augsburg Press, 1981).

30. Anselmo, "Dealing with Stress."

31. Ibid.

## Chapter 19: The Doctor

32. Alsdurf and Alsdurf, *Battered into Submission*, 29.

33. Ibid.

34. Jane O'Reilly, "Wife Beating: The Silent Crime," *Time*, 5 September 1983, 23, cited in Alsdurf and Alsdurf, *Battered into Submission*.

35. Wesley R. Monfalcone, *Coping with Abuse in the Family* (Philadelphia: Westminster Press, 1980), 92–93.

36. Ibid., 93–96.

37. Alexander Lowen, M.D., *Love, Sex, and Your Heart* (New York: Macmillan Publishing, 1988).

## Chapter 20: The Affair

38. Les Carter, *The Prodigal Spouse: How to Survive Infidelity* (Nashville: Thomas Nelson, 1990).

## Chapter 22: The Reconciliation

39. Johnny Jones, comp., *Life Support Leader's Handbook: Your Church's Lifeline to Hurting People*, Life Support Series (Nashville: LifeWay Press, 1993).

## Chapter 24: The Healing

40. M. Scott Peck, M.D., *The Road Less Travelled: A New Psychology of Love, Traditional Values and Spiritual Growth* (New York: Simon and Schuster, 1978), 15.

41. Three excellent resources for doing this are: Richard J. Foster, *Celebration of Discipline* (San Francisco: Harper San Francisco, 1988); Richard J. Foster, *Prayer: Finding the Heart's True Home* (San Francisco: Harper San Francisco, 1992); and Donald G. Bloesch, *The Struggle of Prayer* (Colorado Springs: Helmers and Howard, 1988).

Guy Greenfield, a former college and seminary professor and pastor, is director of The Family Growth Center, a pastoral counseling and family-life education center, in Hereford, Texas. A graduate of Oklahoma Baptist University and Texas Tech University, Greenfield also attended Southwestern Baptist Theological Seminary where he received the masters of divinity degree and the Ph. D. in Christian ethics. He holds the Clinical Pastoral Education Certificate from Palm Beach County Mental Health Hospital. He also holds Pastoral Affiliate Status in the American Association of Pastoral Counselors. He is a charter member of the American Association of Christian Counselors.

Guy and his wife, Carole, have been married for forty-three years and are the parents of three children.